A New Look at
Log Cabin Quilts

DESIGN A SCENE BLOCK BY BLOCK PLUS 9 EASY-TO-FOLLOW PROJECTS

FLAVIN GLOVER

 C&T PUBLISHING

Text and photography ©2003 Flavin Glover

Artwork ©2003 C&T Publishing

Editor-in-Chief: Darra Williamson

Editor: Candie Frankel

Technical Editors: Gailen Runge, Joyce Engels Lytle

Copy Editor: Eva Simoni Erb

Proofreader: Carol Barret

Cover Designer: Kristen Yenche

Design Director/Book Designer: Kristen Yenche

Illustrators: Luke Mulks, Gailen Runge

Production Assistant: Jeff Carrillo

Photographs: Travel photographs and quilt photographs on pages 8, 11, 44 and 52 by Glenn R. Glover. All other quilt photographs, including close-ups, by Sharon Risedorph. Fabric and how-to photographs by C&T staff.

Published by C&T Publishing, Inc., P.O. Box 1456, Lafayette, California 94549

Front cover: *Row Houses* (partial view) by Flavin Glover

Back cover: *Moms and Babes* and *Geese in Flight*, both by Flavin Glover

All rights reserved. No part of this work covered by the copyright hereon may be reproduced and used in any form or by any means—graphic, electronic, or mechanical, including photocopying, recording, taping, or information storage and retrieval systems—without written permission of the publisher. The copyrights on individual artworks are retained by the artists as noted in *A New Look at Log Cabin Quilts*.

Attention Copy Shops: Please note the following exception—Publisher and author give permission to photocopy the log cutting guides and pages 73 and 107 for personal use only.

Attention Teachers: C&T Publishing, Inc. encourages you to use this book as a text for teaching. Contact us at 800-284-1114 or www.ctpub.com for more information about the C&T Teachers Program.

We take great care to ensure that the information included in this book is accurate and presented in good faith, but no warranty is provided nor results guaranteed. Since we have no control over the choices of materials or procedures used, neither the author nor C&T Publishing, Inc. shall have any liability to any person or entity with respect to any loss or damage caused directly or indirectly by the information contained in this book. For your convenience, we post an up-to-date listing of corrections on our website (www.ctpub.com). If a correction is not already noted, please contact our customer service department at ctinfo@ctpub.com or at P.O. Box 1456, Lafayette, CA 94549.

Trademarked (™) and Registered Trademark (®) names are used throughout this book. Rather than use the symbols with every occurrence of a trademark and registered trademark name, we are using the names only in the editorial fashion and to the benefit of the owner, with no intention of infringement.

Library of Congress Cataloging-in-Publication Data

Glover, Flavin.

A new look at log cabin quilts : design a scene block by block plus 9 easy-to-follow projects / Flavin Glover.

p. cm.

ISBN 1-57120-204-8 (paper trade)

1. Patchwork--Patterns. 2. Quilting--Patterns. 3. Log cabin quilts. I. Title.

TT835.G59 2003

746.46'041--dc21

2003002509

Printed in the USA

10 9 8 7 6 5 4 3 2 1

Acknowledgments

■ *Thanks to my husband, Glenn, for his constant support as well as his computer expertise and photography skills.*

■ *Thanks to my sisters, who taught me to sew.*

■ *Thanks to Vonda Lee Waldrep, a neighbor at the farm in North Alabama who showed me her hand-pieced Log Cabin quilt over 25 years ago, and took the time that day to draw me a block-piecing diagram.*

■ *Thanks to my first quilt instructors, Bets Ramsey and Mildred Locke, at the Southern Quilt Symposium.*

■ *Thanks to my students. They are supportive and full of creative ideas that in turn fuel my own creative sparks.*

■ *Thanks to my editor, Candie Frankel, for her skillful and keen attention to detail.*

■ *Thanks to my technical editor, Gailen Runge, who consistently brought enthusiasm and optimism to each task, and to Luke Mulks for illustrations.*

■ *Thanks to my designer, Kristen Yenche, for bringing clarity of visual quality to the project.*

■ *Thanks to the staff at C&T Publishing for asking me to write this book.*

Table of
Contents

Introduction

For over 140 years, Log Cabin quilts have been at the heart of American patchwork. This book is about Log Cabins, but not about the quilts recognized and called by names like Barn Raising and Straight Furrows. *A New Look at Log Cabin Quilts* is filled with variety. Each section of the book explores and illustrates ways that Log Cabin blocks can be modified, stretched, and integrated to create images and panoramic landscapes. By building on traditional block characteristics and features, this book cultivates a more diverse perception of Log Cabin patchwork, and provides the steps, skills, and tools needed to design unique quilts.

The book is divided into four key sections. The opening gallery tells how seven Log Cabin landscape quilts came to be. You'll see the photographs that inspired them, hear the stories behind them, and—best of all—you'll come away with some valuable quiltmaking lessons to apply to your own work. The process section describes how to identify potential design sources, develop a working sketch, choose suitable blocks and a grid, and integrate fabrics and colors. In the quilt

section, nine step-by-step project patterns, representing two decades of experimentation, let you experience firsthand how to transform square and rectangular Log Cabin blocks into stylized patchwork landscapes. A closing gallery looks back at my early quilts, pieced in both Log Cabin and other simple patchwork patterns. Each quilt was a step along my learning path.

My quilts reflect my love of the outdoors. Growing up on a farm, I watched and listened as Dad recounted his daily observations. If he spotted a bird nest in tall grass while cutting hay, that area of the pasture was not cut until the fledglings left the nest. Dad taught me the verse,

> *Red sky in morning, sailor take warning*
> *Red sky at night, sailors' delight.*

A red sunset was indeed a welcome sight when fresh-cut hay was on the ground.

Today, I no longer live on a farm, but I still treasure the beauty that comes with a close attachment to the land. My quilts tell stories of places I love. My search for fresh design sources and inspiration has involved my husband, Glenn, as we travel with camera in hand. It's my hope that the unique journey of your life will lead you in a similar way, so that one day soon you are developing quilted scenes and landscapes of your own. Embrace the task. Take it on. With the classic simplicity of the Log Cabin block, you can make it happen.

Flavin Glover
September 22, 2002

Looking Forward:
Lessons from *the* Quilt Gallery

Creating images with Log Cabin quilts gives me an opportunity to stretch Log Cabin patchwork in new directions. Each design has sparked more ideas, and every new block developed leads to other possibilities. The quilts become learning experiences and teaching tools.

Design inspirations come in all shapes, forms, and sizes. A beach umbrella in a sports apparel catalog reminded me of a Kaleidoscope patchwork block. A few days later, the coupon section of the Sunday paper had a colorful yogurt ad—a stylized scene showing the sea, sailboats, sky, and large yogurt containers sitting on the beach. I couldn't get to graph paper fast enough! By nightfall, I had a scale drawing of a beach scene filled with umbrellas. After the thirteen Kaleidoscope block umbrellas were stitched, I drafted a rectangular Courthouse Steps block to fit around the pieced squares for the sandy beach and ocean. Variation blocks let me create the white patchwork sails. Each color palette included many fabrics.

A Day at the Beach, 89½" x 69", 1996. Kaleidoscope and Elongated Courthouse Steps blocks. Machine-pieced, hand-quilted. Cottons, polyester batting.

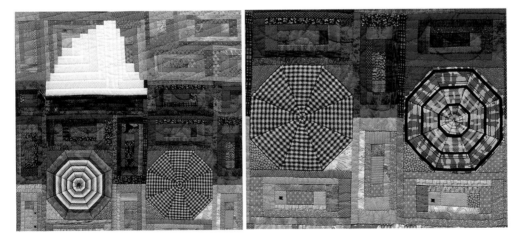

Detail of sailboat and beach umbrellas

Rectangular blocks fit around the umbrellas vertically and horizontally.

LESSONS: Look to everyday items, such as catalogs and advertising circulars, for design inspiration. Simplify your design drawing so that your featured images will stand out and be easy to piece. Use Log Cabin blocks to fill in the spaces around your featured blocks. Rectangular blocks, with their thick and thin log variations, are particularly useful when you design landscapes and scenes.

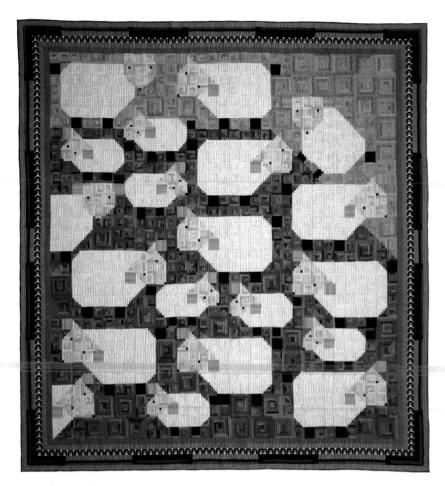

Morning Graze, 96" x 100", 1989. Traditional 2½" x 2½" and 5" x 5" Log Cabin blocks. Machine-pieced, hand-quilted. Cottons and cotton-polyester blends, polyester batting.

In the springtime on New Zealand's South Island, the number of sheep grazing on the steep hillsides or in mountain meadows is astonishing. Staying at a sheep ranch gave us the chance to work with a farmer and his sheep dogs, and to see the ewes and baby lambs up close. A lamb frolics and plays without a care, yet readily responds when its mom calls. Even in a crowded flock where lots of ewes are calling their young, each lamb can hear and find its own mother. Experiencing the scene in person was terrific! We took photographs to document it, and a quilt design was soon in the works.

My first step was to draw a sheep on graph paper. Each square represented a small 2½" x 2½" Log Cabin block. In some areas, a 5" x 5" block would work, replacing four 2½" x 2½" blocks. As I sketched several ewes and lambs on a hillside, the design quickly grew from a wallhanging to a king-size bed quilt. White cotton brocades, which become soft and textured when washed, represent the sheep's woolly coats. This large, heavy quilt is too warm to use in our mild-weather region. Should a freak ice storm ever cause a power outage, we are prepared for a cold night. A smaller sheep quilt, *Moms and Babes*, is featured on page 93.

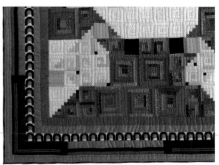

A ewe peeks out from behind the quilt border.

LESSONS: Block sizes that are multiples of one another—such as 2½" x 2½", 5" x 5", 7½" x 7½", and 10" x 10"—fit together like building blocks in a Log Cabin grid. When you're drafting a Log Cabin design to scale, believe the math. The quilt really will be as large as the numbers indicate.

Look up! At a hot air balloon festival, color and design ideas literally float across the sky. A balloon's circular shape is easy to adapt to a Log Cabin quilt. Even a stylized balloon shape with stair-stepped edges can still be recognized, especially if the colors form a brilliant, bold contrast against the background. My initial attempts to use large blocks were unsuccessful. When I reduced the block size to 4" x 4" and used classic Log Cabin block layouts, the balloons took shape. By using small blocks to create a large shape, I was able to add detail and repetition without resorting to appliqué. The blue and yellow balloon incorporates Sunshine and Shadows, and the dazzling red and blue balloon uses Streak of Lightning. I used a traditional Log Cabin block grid with no variation in block size or log width.

Streak of Lightning balloon

Fourth of July balloon chase near Canton, Mississippi

Sunshine and Shadows balloon

Chasing the Wind, 78" x 92", 1982. Traditional Log Cabin blocks. Machine-pieced, hand-quilted. Cottons and cotton-polyester blends, polyester batting.

Lessons: Traditional block layouts such as Barn Raising, Sunshine and Shadows, Straight Furrows, and Streak of Lightning can be incorporated into new Log Cabin designs. When you want movement in a simple, repetitive block layout, the light and dark halves permit numerous setting variations.

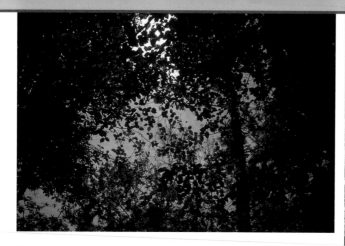

Spring

Autumn

Seasons Ever Changing, 92" x 110", 1983. Traditional Log Cabin blocks in a diagonal set. Machine-pieced, hand-quilted. Cottons and cotton-polyester blends, polyester batting.

LESSONS: When a simple design isn't taking shape on a Log Cabin grid, turn the grid 45° to create a diagonal set. Divisions move vertically through blocks that are set on point, allowing color changes to move up and down through the quilt. Use the power of repetition to accent simple, stylized shapes. Keep the block size small to allow enough design repeats to make an impact.

Photographing trees in all seasons lets me in on a secret: there is color even in winter. A group of gray hardwood tree trunks sparkled in the wintry sunlight. In autumn, there is more color blending, as well as spectacular examples of colors that stand out and show off. When I drive through the eastern Tennessee forests in spring, I enjoy dozens of shades of green as the leaves break bud. If only the blending of green fabrics could be as striking!

This quilt uses trees to represent the four seasons. Each row (and each column) shows one yearly cycle. Turning a basic square grid on the diagonal lets me carry out the tree motif using Log Cabin blocks. Color changes from one tree to the next accomplished the seasonal variations.

Winter

Detail of steep mountain

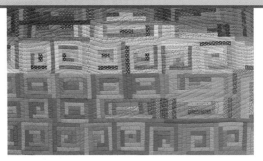

Detail of contour quilting

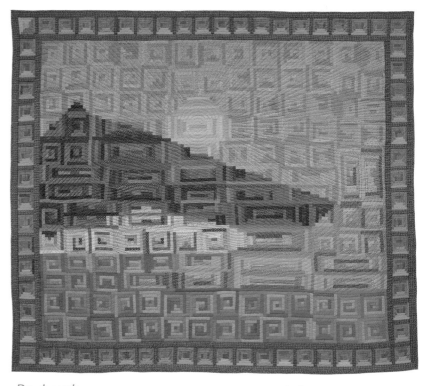

Daybreak, 84" x 98", 1983. Various rectangular and square Log Cabin blocks. Machine-pieced, hand-quilted. Cottons and cotton-polyester blends, polyester batting.

The challenge of this Log Cabin landscape was figuring out how to design the shape of the sun and the varying slopes of the mountains. To depict inclines other than 45°, I elongated the Log Cabin blocks. Placing elongated blocks horizontally creates a gentle slope. Turned vertically, the same block becomes a steep incline. A scale drawing became my design map, enabling me to fit several different block designs and sizes together with ease and accuracy. This preplanned piecing route allowed me to maintain orientation, keep track of block placement, and pinpoint where I had left off. Several months into the project, the design map gave others the illusion that I knew what I was doing!

LESSONS: The position of a rectangular block—horizontal or vertical—affects the slope of its diagonal line. Once the picture takes shape, let those piecing contours generate ideas for the quilting. Quilt across the surface of the blocks, ignoring the patchwork, to depict agricultural contours, mountain slopes, or sunrays across the sky.

Crater Lake, Oregon

Leaves and berries became quilting designs.

LESSONS: A composite drawing lets you incorporate design ideas from multiple photographs and sources. In an imaginary landscape, you easily can adapt Log Cabin blocks in various shapes and sizes to make color and contour changes. Once you create the composite drawing, you can use it as a road map to create an enlarged scale drawing for even finer detail.

When Glenn learned I was invited to teach in Alaska, he quickly reached for his calendar to keep the dates clear. While I taught, he fished! I didn't complain (too much) because the three-week trip was peppered with excursions and holidays from the classroom. Our tour of Alaska provided one glorious natural sight after another. Everywhere I looked—up and down—I found countless design inspirations. Instead of trying for a realistic view of a single area, I pulled all of these images, experiences, recollections, and photographs together into a composite drawing. Distilling my imaginary landscape into a design I could interpret with Log Cabin blocks tested my skills at simplification. I ended up using 232 blocks, in a variety of sizes and log widths, to define and fill out the landscape. Smaller motifs such as animal tracks, snowflakes, salmon, and ferns became quilting designs.

Inside Passage, 88" x 94", 1990. Various rectangular and square Log Cabin blocks. Machine-pieced, hand-quilted. Cottons and cotton-polyester blends, polyester batting.

Appliquéd village

Quilting on back reveals animal tracks.

Glacier Bay on a cloudy day

Lush ferns

Late afternoon sky

Fields of Plenty, 56" x 40", 1986. Asymmetrical patchwork and Rectangular Courthouse Steps blocks. Machine-pieced, hand-quilted. Cottons, polyester batting.

LESSONS: To design a landscape with an aerial view, raise the horizon line and let the lines of perspective fan out generously. The idea is to make the fields in the foreground, or lower part of the quilt, appear much larger than the fields in the background. Color changes can separate one field from another without the need for additional patchwork. Use repetitive quilting to create plowed rows and furrows, clouds, and subtle movement throughout the design.

Aerial view of farmland

Fields of Plenty creates the illusion of depth, distance, and endless vista. Seemingly parallel lines converge at an imaginary point beyond the horizon, making the fields that are closest to the sky appear miles away. When you walk by this quilt, the most distant fields seem to stay with you, while those in the foreground pass by at a steady pace. I put the principles of perspective to work, using an aerial view of farmland as a design source. Repetitive quilting lines and assorted earthy colors add to the mix, giving a realistic aura to the fields. I happened to watch the movie *Top Gun* while this design idea was cooking. Seeing the pilot's careening view of the horizon as the fighter jet banked right and left gave me one more idea. I gently tilted the quilt grid a few degrees, just enough to alter the perspective so that the visual plane was no longer flat. With the diagonal lines off-kilter, I suddenly found myself part of a dynamic "interactive" design. I have watched people turn their heads sideways—and then sideways some more—as they try to take in the scene while regaining their equilibrium.

Fields meet sky.

All around you, potential quilt designs lie dormant, waiting to be discovered and developed. It is up to you to **look** for design sources that are meaningful to you. The following section provides helpful considerations as you begin your quest for quilt designs that you can create yourself.

The
Process

Part *1*

Finding Inspiration

Selecting a design source gets the quilt process rolling and focuses your attention on necessary steps. Knowing that you want to create an original quilt is not enough. Something has to trigger the impulse. You won't stay motivated without a topic, a reason, or an inspiration that you deem worthy of your time and effort. Look to see what catches your eye, piques your interest, or leads you into dreaming of a new quilt—and then let that "something" become your inspiration.

The great outdoors abounds with ideas for quilted landscapes. The location doesn't have to be exotic—you might choose the view from your own back porch. Train yourself to watch for design possibilities wherever you are. Look at your environment with open eyes, much the way a weather watcher routinely scans the skies for changing cloud patterns. Cloud cover can reveal or obliterate a magnificent mountain peak in a matter of minutes. An awesome sight suddenly appears, then just as quickly vanishes, demonstrating the dramatic power of light on a landscape. The real joy of going outdoors to seek quilt design inspirations is the journey—to be there, to actually see the things that stir up the creative process. When you learn how to focus on a potential design source, you become more attentive. You absorb the total experience instead of just casually observing it.

A change in perspective lets you see familiar scenes with new eyes. Bend down to look up, or climb up to look down, and you'll get a brand-new take on how something looks, and which features to emphasize. A different vantage point may alter your preconceived ideas about construction, color plan, or style. It can help you determine what elements from the scene to include, or how to interpret them in your patchwork.

Seasonal changes provide bountiful color variations to draw on. On a narrow walking path far from a paved road, I came upon a brilliant display of maple leaves that had fallen and lodged in a bed of ferns. Building on my experience, *Fall's Glow* (page 110) depicts stylized trees in the peak fall color season. I quilted full-sized leaf motifs in each tree, with leaf shapes and fall colors that match the trees' species.

Looking down brings a rich color reward.

Quiltmakers are frequently inspired by architectural motifs, old and new. American quilters are notorious for walking with their heads down on European tours. They intently study ceramic tile floors or mosaic stone wall motifs that were grouted in place hundreds or thousands of years ago. Any tourist is apt to glance down and notice a cathedral's sprawling circular floor mosaic, but quilters are the ones who take in all the intricate details, and track down the obscure block designs that seem to have sashing and border. How can

Looking up at Mt. Cook on New Zealand's South Island

we remember to look up when authentic patchwork patterns lie underfoot?

A stonemason's patchwork mosaic in Pompeii, Italy

Lest you forget the visual riches of your travels, take plenty of photographs and save the travel brochures. Later, these mementos will supplement your memory of a scene or place. Brief notes about color, or a partial sketch on a napkin, can preserve the details as a snapshot records the view.

PHOTOGRAPHS

Photographs give you an opportunity to focus on aspects you might otherwise miss. You might fall in love with a historic building, but it's not until you begin photographing it that you notice the unusual, centuries-old brickwork. Taking your own photographs sharpens your eye, and gives you a design source that is unique to you. Whatever intrigues you—sunrises, sunsets, lighthouses, sailboats—photograph it. Systematically photographing things you appreciate or adore will give you lots of visual references to draw on for your quilt designs.

Another approach is to photograph the unlikely subject. For instance, some hotel rooms have a view and others don't. When you travel, routinely photograph the view, regardless of whether or not you consider it pleasant. A seemingly mundane view may inspire a better quilt design than a stunning view from an expensive room. Photographs not only provide reference to a scene; they refresh your memory and sensory recall when you're developing a quilt design.

The angle from which we mortals view a sight influences our overall perspective. Finding the best place to stand to photograph a breathtaking scene, such as the patchwork farmland high in the Andes Mountains, does make a difference. Different people have different opinions about the ideal angle for a photograph. Glenn, my husband and shutterbug partner, resolved this issue long ago. He will shoot his view and mine; often, he will shoot the same scene from multiple locations or vantage points, using different lenses or camera settings. Thanks to his camera skills, our travels have brought me countless inspirations for quilt design.

Don't be discouraged by your seeming lack of photographic skills. The hour of day, the sun's angle, and the weather all affect a photograph's quality. Couple these natural variables with a tight time schedule, or a vehicle that suddenly motors into your picture frame, and you'll be hard-pressed to take the "ideal" photograph. Get what you can, rather than taking no picture at all! For every good picture you take, expect several mediocre ones. Get used to this fact, and compensate by taking several shots of each potential design inspiration. Even poor pictures can serve as a catalyst or inspiration. You aren't required to document the photograph in your quilt—you can change a cloudy, rainy day into a sunny one, or easily remove a power line. Photographs often provide more detail than you need, and may benefit from cropping. Don't hesitate to use only a portion of a picture.

"There is no way a picture can do this justice!" This is the remark I repeatedly overheard as I stood 12,500 feet above sea level, overlooking a grand and spectacular view in the Andes Mountains. Photos can capture only a certain degree of depth. The privilege of looking out and enjoying such scenery in all its splendor is a gift.

Some quiltmakers embrace the challenge of translating such depth of view into a quilt, while for others it remains only a dream. Designing a quilt inspired from such a breathtaking view seems audacious, yet humbling; unrealistic, yet amazingly possible.

View of neighboring villages from Quesimpuco, Bolivia

Your Camera

Take inspirational photos with whatever camera you choose—a 35mm camera with an array of sophisticated lenses, an automatic point-and-shoot camera, a digital camera, or an inexpensive disposable camera. Base your equipment options on what you already own and are comfortable using. Any option will work! Digital cameras, scanners, and computers extend the ways a design source can be adapted.

Fields first cultivated centuries ago appear like patchwork in a remote region of Bolivia's Andes Mountains.

PUBLICATIONS

Students often come to class with travel magazines, postcards, and lavish tourist brochures filled with picture-perfect views of the places they have visited. Seeing my students' hand-picked collections gives me clues about their interests, passions, and identity. My goal is to teach students how to channel the designs they love into creative drawings and, ultimately, unique quilts.

Tourist publications make the perfect complement to personal photographs. They offer another design source to tap for scene and color ideas. Your notion of a blue sky may fade when you consider a postcard's vibrant orange, pink, coral, and red sunset.

While I rarely use magazine or calendar photographs for direct inspiration, I find them excellent for design exercises and teaching tools. I use them to assist students who are learning how to problem-solve, and how to adapt buildings or scenes to Log Cabin patchwork. Being able to assess a design is just as important as learning how to adapt one. A quick sketch of a lovely national park vista seen on a calendar may convince both student and teacher that the view doesn't lend itself to a Log Cabin landscape. Why waste time fussing over a troublesome design when hundreds of more user-friendly possibilities await you?

YOUR IMAGINATION

Another way to come up with or augment an inspiration for a quilt is to tap into your imaginative powers. Imaginative thoughts about a design can occur even when no sketch or photograph exists. When you allow your imagination to mix the various aspects of quilt designing, you'll be ready to take advantage of all the sensory material that comes your way. Your ideas for colors, fabrics, block design, construction methods, and quilting stitches will always be close to the surface, ready to spring into action when you need them to fulfill a design vision.

To keep track of all your ideas, start a design folder. A design folder can be virtual within a computer or it can be a tangible folder holding such items as paint chips, line drawings of blocks, fabric swatches, photographs, sketches, and doodles. Filling a design folder is similar to building a fabric stash. Both are investments in future creative quilt work.

Close-up of tundra bearberries

Doodling

Allowing yourself to sketch or doodle just for the fun of it is a good habit for a quilter. A pencil or a computer mouse can be the primary drawing tool. Go ahead. Jot down an idea. Draw a shape on graph paper. Make a picture as realistic or as abstract as you choose. If you get a sudden inspiration, record your idea while it's clear and fresh, so you can keep that potential quilt alive. If you feel stuck, set the drawing aside and come back to it later. Time away from a drawing is often necessary for a concept to fully emerge. A design solution in the form of a cluster of buildings, a grove of trees, or a historic lighthouse may come to mind when you least expect it.

Here's an example of the type of imaginative design building I'm talking about. I experienced a marvelous display of color while hiking along a footpath in Denali National Park in Alaska. The tundra was covered with glowing plants. Clouds formed, then instantly dissipated atop stately Mt. McKinley. Looking up and looking down provided lots of inspiration. By using my imagination and photographs to recall the total experience, I was able to articulate several design opportunities. Here are my notes:

- Select fabrics with visual texture in both warm colors and deep, cool colors to capture the tundra in autumn.

- Find fabrics with circular motifs for instant detail quilting lines in the tundra.

- Establish two white fabric palettes: one with texture and sheen for the snow, and the other with soft pastel blue streaks (explore hand-dyed fabrics) for the sky and clouds.

- Pull the foreground or base of the design forward to distort the scale. In addition to using color contrasts, vary the log widths and block sizes to promote spatial depth. Mt. McKinley's grandeur, even when depicted far in the distance, will counterbalance the enlarged foreground.

Tundra in Denali National Park viewed against Mount McKinley

Developing a Design

Each quilt presents its own unique design problems and opportunities. There are no specific guidelines that work every time. One design drawing may come together with ease, while the next one presents numerous obstacles that may or may not reach a resolution in Log Cabin patchwork. Quilt design isn't so much a linear process, where one step is completed before the next one is initiated, as it is a juggling act. Because decisions made along the way influence how everything comes together, you have to train yourself to think about and visualize the entire project from the very beginning. In this chapter, we'll look at techniques for translating inspirational photos into quilt designs. As you'll see, the key is to think creatively about a lot more than just the immediate step at hand.

SKETCHES

The first step is to translate the inspirational photo into a simple line drawing. Work with pencil and plain paper, or onscreen with drawing software and a mouse. The idea is to separate one design area from another. Keeping the sketch simple makes it possible to determine quickly whether there is a foreground, a middle ground, and a background. If the design doesn't break out naturally into three distinct areas, no problem. But if it does, you can use these "natural" color breaks later on to enhance spatial perspective or to change the scale of logs or blocks.

Students frequently ask where to begin a sketch. If there is a horizon or another horizontal dividing line, draw it. Examples include the base of a mountain, the dividing line between water and sky, a fence, a lakeshore, or a road. Then draw in the other major features. If there are mountains, try to capture the slope or incline. A cityscape may have one central building or a prominent landmark.

Allow that feature to become the anchor, and then draw in other buildings or features to scale.

A float ride down the Colorado River through Glen Canyon provided a stunning inspirational photograph for a Log Cabin landscape. The photograph had easy-to-draw shapes, foreground, middle ground, background, and strong areas of naturalistic colors. Your first sketch should be a bare-bones rendering, keeping only the essential shapes that attracted you in the first place. The more details you can eliminate, the more likely the scene will be adaptable to a Log Cabin interpretation. It's a good sign if the completed sketch looks similar to the photo that inspired it.

On the Colorado River in Glen Canyon, Arizona

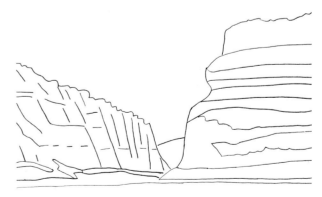

A first sketch of the Glen Canyon photo

A second, more developed sketch

LOOK

Colored Pencils

Colored pencils can quickly divide shapes on a sketch, indicate areas of contrast, and give a sense of proportion. Think of colored pencils as a design tool. They won't give you an accurate color picture of the finished quilt, but they can help you plan your approach and work creatively on problem areas.

A second sketch lets you fine-tune the design. Will you use square or rectangular Log Cabin blocks? Designing with straight logs and blocks has limitations. Shapes tend to be blocky. Smooth, curved lines are practically nonexistent. Here's where you'll begin auditioning different block arrangements, or grids, to determine which ones best suit the design. Adding color to the sketch defines the various areas of transition more clearly. In the next two chapters, we'll look more closely at different blocks and how to use them to carry out a design.

Working out a practical grid pattern for a design takes time, so keep your options open. Expect the sketch to change as you problem-solve and try out design alternatives. Keep in mind that fabric choices, color changes within fabrics, and quilting stitches—things that you can't easily depict on your sketch—can help you over a design hurdle later in the process. If you're flexible, willing to stylize images, and not afraid to experiment, you can adapt a favorite landscape, a building, a flower garden, or any special idea into Log Cabin patchwork.

COMPOSITE DRAWINGS

If an inspiration doesn't offer a complete design, you may want to combine elements from many inspirations. Sometimes, try as you might, that single perfect photograph never materializes. You visit a location and take numerous photos, but none of them captures the full view or the ambiance you remember.

Sketching allows you to select features from various design sources and merge them into one drawing. Composite drawings can really pack a punch. A few minutes of creativity is all it takes to move mountains, divert rivers, and relocate prime real estate—before you know it, your new imaginary landscape is on the map. Composite sketches are also useful when you want to pull images together and adjust the design lines to fit a particular block grid or combination.

Traveling to the ghost town of Bodie, near Bridgeport, California, was like discovering gold for me. To walk about the dusty streets of such an authentic environment was a photographer's dream. I was constantly challenged to capture on film the essence of what I saw. It was easy to photograph head-on views of individual buildings, but being at ground level with a narrow field of vision limited the role my camera could play. I wanted to photograph clusters of buildings from above. If only I'd had temporary scaffolding. If only a regional electric boom truck would have cruised into Bodie right then!

Dozens of Bodie photographs await my attention for a future quilt design. Pulling the buildings together into a composite drawing, without regard to the town map and street grid, got me over the first hurdle. Enjoyable challenges remain, such as finding suitable fabrics, determining which buildings to emphasize, and designing block variations to integrate all the patchwork.

Bodie State Historic Park has numerous vintage buildings.

A composite drawing based on the Bodie photographs

TACKLING THE PRIORITIES

Once you have a working sketch, focus your attention on the important features of the design. A key design feature often dictates the flow or orientation (vertical or horizontal) of a quilt design. The flow or orientation, in turn, may affect how you develop the block grid design. You want to start thinking about how you might render these key features, because your entire design rests upon them.

Begin by comparing your sketch to the original design source, to be sure that you preserved essential or desired aspects of the design. Rank the details in order of importance if you are unsure which to keep and which to omit. An image that sets the tone of the scene is worth keeping, but small details that would be difficult to depict might not be. Size isn't always an accurate indicator of importance. In *Geese in Flight* (page 65), the Canada geese are relatively small, but they are vital to the design. Finding an easy way to render them realistically became my priority when I was developing this design. Once I had the goose construction figured out, I was free to go ahead with the block grid.

If an aspect of the design has you stumped, think outside the box. You don't *have* to use Log Cabin blocks for a featured image. Other patchwork shapes, appliqué, surface embellishment, and quilting can also bring an idea to life. Shapes that are suggestive, rather than laden with details, can be quite successful, and are also easier to render. Clumps of green, for instance, may be sufficient to indicate a distant forest. You can dispense with worrying about how to depict branches, leaves, and needles.

If a sketch includes a vast landscape or cityscape, cropping in on a smaller area can keep the piecing manageable, while still retaining enough detail to make the design visually interesting. Photographs taken from a hotel window in La Paz, Bolivia, illustrate this point. The overall view showed centuries of patched construction, appearing wonderfully chaotic and haphazard.

View from a hotel room in LaPaz, Bolivia

When I zoomed in for a closer look, I discovered an orange tabby cat looking back at me with shared amusement. Should this inspiration become a quilt design, the cat will have high priority, along with the multiple angles in the architecture.

Zooming in on an orange tabby cat

DRAWING TO SCALE

Once you've completed a sketch and evaluated the special design issues, it's time to move the design onto a grid. As before, you can use pencil and graph paper, or you can work onscreen, using your mouse as a drawing tool. Mistakes aren't an issue. Pencil marks can be erased. With a computer, you can make unwanted lines vanish with the click of a button.

A scale drawing offers many benefits. It acts like a road map, identifying twists and turns that aren't apparent on the sketch. It gives you a more extensive preview of the potential quilt, allowing you to work out a color scheme and plan colors to enhance depth. You foresee problems early in the process, thus saving time, fabric, and aggravation. The grid forces the drawing into components suitable for conventional patchwork, and allows you to count the number of blocks you'll need.

As in all patchwork, the size of the blocks determines the size of the finished quilt. If each finished log is ½" wide, each round of logs will add 1" to the block size. If each finished log is 1" wide, each round will add 2" to the block, and so forth. How wide to make the logs, and how many rounds of logs to use in a block, depends on the level of detail your subject requires. Each quilt design is unique. *Chasing the Wind* (page 7) and *Seasons Ever Changing* (page 8) both use 4" blocks, but the log widths and number of rows in the blocks are different for each quilt.

A scale drawing needn't be large—most designs can fit on an 8½" x 11" sheet. But if a quilt is very large or uses lots of block variations, expanding the design onto a larger sheet of graph paper is worth the extra time and effort. An enlarged, detailed drawing allows you to nail down the details, problem-solve a block's internal color changes, count blocks and logs with precision, and confirm their orientation.

Another way to assess the details is by enlarging only those blocks that are directly involved. To make *Moms and Babes* (page 93), I worked mainly from a scale drawing of the entire quilt, but I drew actual-sized blocks on graph paper to figure out the lambs' eyes and noses.

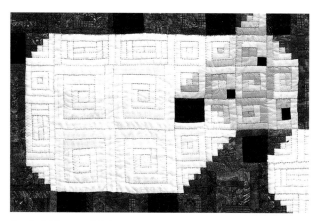

Detail of *Moms and Babes*

The beauty of drawing a Log Cabin grid to scale is that it will enlarge to its full size with ease and accuracy. If a scale drawing is balanced and has good proportions, so will the full-scale quilt. If a drawing seems lopsided or top-heavy, it's relatively easy to fix, compared to the seam-ripping, fabric-wasting alternative. Always pay attention to trouble spots in the drawing. If left unresolved, they will only loom larger in the quilt.

Sew-By-Number

When you finish your scale drawing, slip the page into a clear plastic sheet protector. Number the blocks consecutively by writing directly on the transparent cover with a permanent fine-point marker. Number your completed blocks to correspond, using self-stick reusable labels (I prefer the Avery brand). Mark a small arrow on the label to indicate the block orientation.

A Design Exercise

✓ Start with an inspirational photo, such as the well-framed view of Lake Tahoe shown here.

✓ Sketch the scene, breaking it down into simple components and major design lines.

✓ Work some color into the sketch to further distinguish the shapes.

✓ Adapt the sketch to a grid of square or rectangular Log Cabin blocks. Let the stepped logs within the blocks represent the major design lines.

✓ Draw the grid to scale on graph paper, and fine-tune the design.

Square Blocks

Triangles, diamonds, and hexagons are all possibilities with Log Cabin piecing, but the basic shape—the starting point for all Log Cabin enthusiasts—remains the square. Square blocks are easy to piece, and can be readily adapted to a grid. This chapter looks at five square blocks. Each block offers a different way of fitting the logs together, and these variations provide the options for creating pictorial images.

TRADITIONAL LOG CABIN BLOCK

In a traditional Log Cabin block, the rectangular patches, or logs, build out from a center log in an organized way. The center log is labeled A, and the surrounding logs are labeled B, C, D, E, and so on through the alphabet. In addition to identifying the logs, the letters indicate the piecing route. In a traditional block, the piecing route can proceed either clockwise (as shown here) or counterclockwise. As new logs are added in concentric rounds, rows of logs radiate off the center. The logs create an evenly stepped pattern that reaches out to the four corners. These "stair steps" divide the block into quadrants.

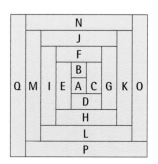

Block Diagram

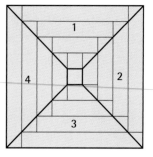

Viewed as Quadrants

What this block can do:

■ **Divide a square into light/dark halves.** Light logs are used in two adjacent quadrants and dark logs in the two remaining quadrants. Determining the quadrants to emphasize is an exercise in movement and color play. Classic design layouts, often used in bed quilts and wallhangings, have recognized names, as discussed in *Chasing the Wind* (page 7).

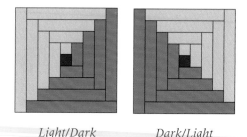

Light/Dark   *Dark/Light*

■ **Contain the color.** A single fabric is used for each round (for example, logs B, C, D, and E). The resulting pattern, called White House Steps, prevents diagonal movement through the block. White House Steps lets you gradate color values within a block, from light to dark or from dark to light. The pattern makes frugal use of fabrics, something to keep in mind when choices or colors are limited.

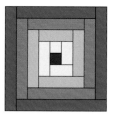
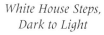

White House Steps,
Light to Dark

White House Steps,
Dark to Light

■ **Rotate with ease.** Quadrant 1 has the shortest outside log, Quadrant 4 has the longest log, and quadrants 2 and 3 fall in the middle. These differences, while slight, are useful. The entire block can be flipped or rotated, repositioning the quadrants to aid the quilt design. Rotating the block 90°, so that Quadrant 4 is in 12 o'clock position, allows logs M and Q to become the hull of a sailboat. Appliquéd sails complete the image.

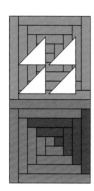

A Sailboat

More Ideas

Log A is a large yellow rectangle—perfect for depicting windows in a row house.

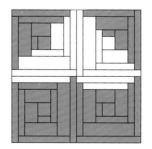

Multiwidth logs in blue and white suggest puffy clouds. Incremental changes in the log widths, such as ½", ¾" or 1", keep the math easy.

OFFSET CENTER LOG CABIN BLOCK

In an Offset Center Log Cabin block, Log A is in one corner, and the logs build out on two sides. The construction is less stable than in the traditional block. Extra care is required to avoid pulling or distorting the logs.

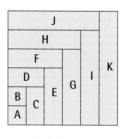

Block Diagram

What this block can do:

■ **Depict a tree.** Turn the block on point with Log A at the bottom to represent a trunk, hidden by the branches.

A Fir Tree

■ **Depict leaves or a flower blossom.** Turn the block on point with Log A at the top to depict leaves or palm fronds. For a flower in full bloom, make Log A larger.

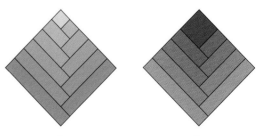

A Leafy Stem   *A Flower*

- **Create diagonal movement.** Group several blocks together to create strong diagonal movement, such as the rows and furrows in a field.

Diagonal Lines

OFFSET CENTER VARIATION BLOCK

In this block, Log A is positioned somewhere between the center of the block and a corner. The remaining logs are sewn concentrically around Log A, just as in a traditional Log Cabin block. The square dimensions are achieved by using wide logs in two adjacent quadrants and narrow logs in the two remaining quadrants. Each quadrant has the same number of logs.

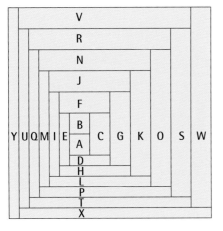

Block Diagram

What this block can do:

- **Introduce curved lines.** Instead of a straight diagonal, the stair steps move through the block in a gentle curve. Single blocks can be effectively inserted into a grid of square blocks to make "round" shapes, such as a sun or moon. Join multiple blocks together for serpentine movement.

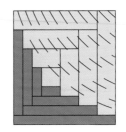

A Corner Sun

- **Create dynamic secondary shapes.** The curves multiply when the blocks are joined in quadrants. Use this approach to create intriguing four-pointed stars. Turn the quadrants on-point to make a butterfly.

Four-Pointed Star

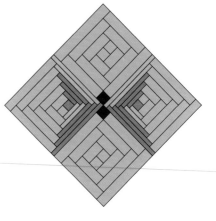

Butterfly

More Ideas

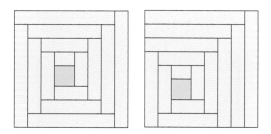

These offset center blocks feature the same log width throughout. The log count varies by quadrant to maintain the square dimensions. Use this variation to position diagonal stair-stepped lines exactly where you need them in the quilt layout.

COURTHOUSE STEPS BLOCK

In a Courthouse Steps block, logs are joined in pairs to opposite edges of the center unit. The block builds out from the center, alternating from side to side. The result is that opposite quadrants are identical: Quadrants 1 and 3 match, as do quadrants 2 and 4.

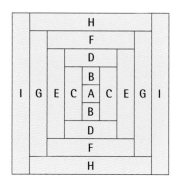

Block Diagram

What this block can do:

■ **Make simple circular shapes.** Join two blocks at quadrants 1 and 4 to make the diagonal lines read as a sun or moon. Choose different fabrics in the same shade to add piecing interest.

Quadrants 1 and 4 form a sun.

■ **Multiply into colorful Japanese lanterns.** A bright, vibrant, multicolored palette can be quickly transformed into a light show. Logs in adjoining quadrants are cut from the same fabric to achieve this effect.

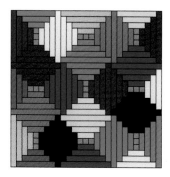

Japanese Lanterns

CORNERSTONES LOG CABIN BLOCK

The Cornerstones block features one Log A in the center and additional Log A "cornerstones" at the ends of specified logs. The cornerstones are joined to their respective logs first, and the piecing continues in alphabetical order from there. The cornerstones form a strong diagonal pattern across the block.

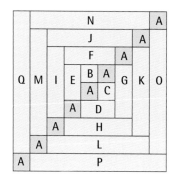

Block Diagram

What this block can do:

- **Keep your eyes moving across the quilt.**

- **Divide the block in half diagonally.** The diagonal pattern allows for three distinct color areas. In *Up at Sunrise* (page 56), the cornerstones become the ropes for a hot air balloon. In the block shown here, the logs on the right are the gondola basket and those on the left are meadows.

A Gondola Rope

- **Divide the block in quadrants.** Run the cornerstones from corner to corner in both directions. This pattern is called Chimneys and Cornerstones.

Chimneys and Cornerstones

- **Create secondary designs.** Cornerstones cut from a contrasting fabric appear superimposed on the background. They can be used to represent freestanding structures like windmills or the trusses in suspension bridges.

More Ideas

Traditional Log Cabin block with three cornerstones becomes a small pine tree when turned on point.

Four cornerstones make up a flower stem in this Offset Center Log Cabin block.

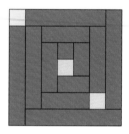

Randomly placed cornerstones represent buttercups in a meadow.

Cornerstones as a Lamb's Eyes and Nose

Rectangular Blocks

Square blocks are the ticket to stair-stepped diagonals and modified circles. Rectangular blocks let us stretch out those sloping curves horizontally and vertically into parabolic swirls. This chapter features four blocks to incorporate into your Log Cabin quilt designs.

RECTANGULAR COURTHOUSE STEPS BLOCK

If you make Log A oblong, you can stretch a square Courthouse Steps block into a rectangle. The extent to which the center log "grows" determines the proportions of the new block. This version uses a 2:1 ratio. When the logs are ¾" wide, Log A is 1½" long; when the logs are 1" wide, Log A is 2" long, and so forth. As in a square Courthouse Steps block, the logs in quadrants 1 and 3 are the same length, and the quadrants fall in mirror image. Likewise, quadrants 2 and 4 are mirror images. Add as many log rounds as you desire.

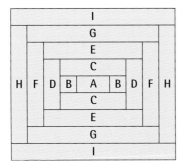

Block Diagram

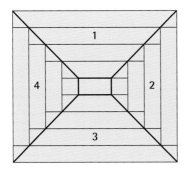

Viewed as Quadrants

What this block can do:

■ **Break out of the mold** with shapes that aren't square and quadrants that aren't angled at 45°.

■ **Influence color position.** Quadrants 1 and 3 have longer logs than quadrants 2 and 4. This affects how the light and dark colors fall, and significantly alters the overall color flow.

Quadrants 1 and 3 are dark.

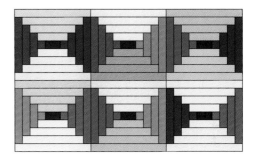

Quadrants 2 and 4 are dark.

ELONGATED COURTHOUSE STEPS BLOCK

This rectangular block is twice as long as it is wide. The logs build out from the center in pairs, alternating between narrow and wide logs. In the 10" x 5" block on page 28, there are four rounds total. The logs are ½" and 1" wide. At the center, two 1" x 1" A logs appear side by side. The A logs seem to join with the other wide logs in the block, separating and dividing the narrow logs into two separate groups.

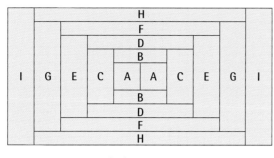

Block Diagram

What this block can do:

- ■ **Sit horizontally or vertically.** Elongated blocks can be stacked horizontally or vertically as the quilt design dictates. In *Daybreak* (page 9), horizontal blocks make up the sea and vertical blocks make up the steep mountain incline.

- ■ **Fit into a square grid.** A 10" x 5" block can fit with two 5" x 5" blocks in a square grid.

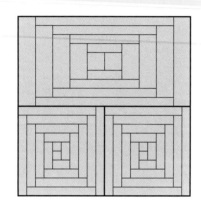

Fitting Blocks Together

- ■ **Establish a half-shift.** The half-shift staggers the block placement and breaks up a rigid block layout. You don't have to match the corner seams! Try the half-shift for skies, seas, and meadows. Start and end every other row with a traditional square Log Cabin block to even out the edges. The sky in *A Day at the Beach* (page 5) was set in half-shift.

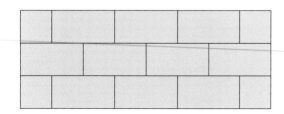

Half-Shift Pattern

More Ideas

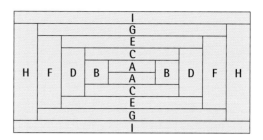

In this 10" x 5" block, each A log is a 2" x ½" rectangle. This small alteration changes the dynamic of the block. The narrow logs become dominant, and the wider logs are pushed off into two distinct groups.

SMALL ELONGATED COURTHOUSE STEPS BLOCK

This smaller rectangular block is useful for filling out a design made up of varying block sizes. A sample size is 5" x 2½", with a finished log width of ½". The stepped pattern is less pronounced than in the larger version.

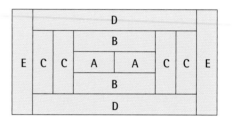

Block Diagram

What this block can do:

- ■ **Sit horizontally or vertically.** Like the larger version, the block can be turned to suit the design.

- ■ **Fill out a design.** Small rectangular blocks can be integrated into the scale drawing wherever needed. In this close-up from the *Moms and Babes* quilt diagram, note how the rectangular blocks fit into the sheep body and green pasture.

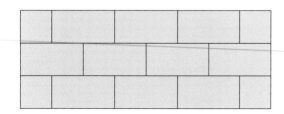

Design Details

■ **Fit into a square grid.** A 5" x 2½" block can fit with two 2½" x 2½" blocks in a square grid.

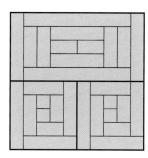

Fitting Blocks Together

More Ideas

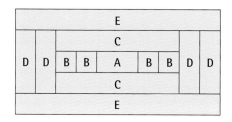

Placing the A's and B's in a single line emphasizes the elongation and changes the stair-step pattern. Devise the block layout to suit your quilt design.

FLEXIBLE-LENGTH COURTHOUSE STEPS BLOCK

This Courthouse Steps block can vary in length, while still maintaining block width. Its flexibility makes it useful for depicting certain shapes. In the following set of blocks, logs C, E, and G remain constant, but logs A, B, D, and F grow progressively longer.

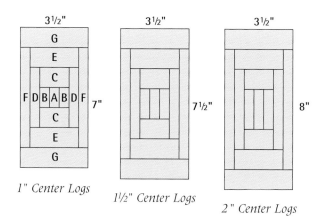

1" Center Logs

1½" Center Logs

2" Center Logs

What this block can do:

■ **Stack vertically, for rows of varying heights.** As long as the block width remains uniform, blocks of varying lengths can stack in vertical columns. I used this adaptation to place the windows and doors in *Carolina Row* (page 88). The differences in length are barely noticeable in the overall grid.

■ **Fill out an awkward grid.** When you don't need Log Share (page 32) for all of the blocks in a row, flexible-length blocks can make up the difference.

More Ideas

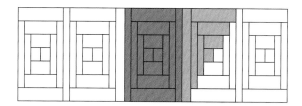

Keeping the block length the same, but stretching the width, is another way to finesse a block shape. Wider blocks depict the tree trunks in the bottom row of Sustainable.

The Block Connection

Stylizing is obviously limited with Log Cabin blocks. As a rule of thumb, the fewer the shapes and images in a Log Cabin design, the better. A simplified drawing, with basic shapes and curves delineated, gives you a sound start. Now you have to find the right blocks to represent those shapes in your Log Cabin quilt top.

FINDING THE RIGHT GRID

The term *grid* refers to the pattern that is formed when lots of blocks are grouped together. Square blocks create one sort of grid pattern. Rectangular blocks have a different look.

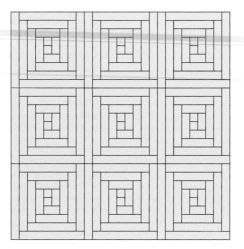

A Square Grid Pattern

A Rectangular Grid Pattern

The simplest approach to designing the quilt top is to select one block size and shape for the grid, and impose that grid over the entire design sketch. Color and fabric variations within the blocks can bring out the sloped or curved lines represented in the sketch.

Look at the design sketch for clues about which block and grid to use. Each block pattern has its own unique characteristics and strong points. By becoming familiar with the different block types and their design capabilities, you'll be able to choose the block and grid that best suits your design. For example, diagonal lines on a 45° angle call for traditional Log Cabin blocks in a square grid. A landscape with a lake in the foreground and gently sloping mountains beyond will more likely fit into elongated rectangular blocks turned horizontally. Head-on views of buildings and townscapes can be built with block quadrants and straight lines, using either squares or rectangles. The grid you choose may depend on which block—square or rectangle—more closely matches the roof slope in your design sketch.

Fudge Factor

When a simple design *almost* matches a grid, try tweaking the design. Redrawing a line or two on your sketch is an easy way to reconcile the practicalities of block construction with your original design vision.

Block Swapping

Sometimes, a solo block pattern simply isn't sufficient to render *all* aspects of the design. In these situations, identify the block and grid pattern that will work for *most* of the design. Then zero in on the problem areas. When a particular block isn't cooperative, substitute a variation that is. As long as the overall block dimensions are the same, you can make as many swaps as you need.

Simply plug the new block into the grid in place of the old one. For example, in a square grid of traditional Log Cabin blocks and Courthouse Steps blocks, you might insert a few variation blocks with multiwidth logs to represent puffy white clouds.

Using Other Patchwork Blocks

Familiar patchwork blocks can be integrated into a Log Cabin grid to aid in depicting shapes. Try Star or Pinwheel blocks for treetops and flower blossoms. In *A Day at the Beach* (page 5), square Kaleidoscope blocks become beach umbrellas. They are surrounded by Rectangular Courthouse Steps blocks. Rail Fence blocks become ears, hoofs, and tails in *Morning Graze* (page 6). Always work out the design for special patchwork blocks first, and then design the Log Cabin blocks to go with them.

A patchwork beach umbrella

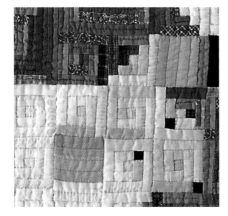

Rail Fence blocks as lamb's ears

Using Appliqué

When details are important but not easy to depict with patchwork logs, appliqué is a viable solution. The village houses and trees in *Inside Passage* (page 10) are appliquéd. The boats in *Seascape* (page 108) have appliquéd sails. In *Geese in Flight* (page 65), the geese wings were strip pieced and then appliquéd to the surface.

Appliquéd village

Appliquéd sails

Appliquéd wings and bellies

Log Share

Log Share is a grid-altering technique that lets you decrease the height or length of a line of rectangular blocks. As the name implies, an outside log is "shared" by two blocks.

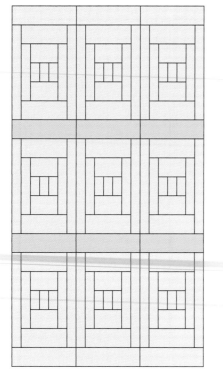

Log Share

Log Share has several applications. It enhances the stair-step effect when the blocks are divided diagonally into light/dark halves. It also gives you a way to shorten the overall block length without changing the length of Log A. *Carolina Row* (page 88) uses Log Share to achieve an aesthetically pleasing pitch to the roof.

The Complex Grid

Some design sketches will never fit a standard block grid—there are too many lines angling off in different directions. A grid that combines square and rectangular blocks of varying sizes can help preserve the twists and turns of the design. You can turn, stack, and resize the blocks until they fit together like a puzzle. When you're done, you'll feel like a genius!

Keep the pencil eraser or delete key on the computer handy as you audition different blocks. For easy integration, use block sizes that are multiples of one another. A 2½" x 2½" square, 5" x 5" square, 10" x 10" square, 2½" x 5" rectangle, and 5" x 10" rectangle are five block sizes that can be fitted together in countless ways. Color changes within the blocks can intensify the sense of motion, as in the sky of *Inside Passage* (page 10).

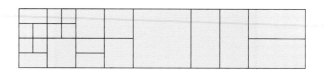

A Complex Grid Plan

Fabrics and Colors

A successful quilt offers interest at many different levels. Color stimulates a first response, when we view the quilt from across the room. As we move closer, the subtle color variations, details in the fabric prints, and individual quilting stitches gain our attention. As the quilt draws us in, we respond to its colors, shapes, patterns, and overall theme on a personal level. The quiltmaker's goal is to incorporate contrast, repetition, and depth over the surface of the quilt in a way that totally mesmerizes the viewer. This creative interplay is achieved primarily through fabric—the quiltmaker's palette.

Colorful "postage stamp" balloons form a repetitive border in *Chasing the Wind* (page 7). The bright border colors counterbalance the large balloon motifs that dominate the quilt.

ASSEMBLING A PALETTE

Students frequently ask how to select fabric, how much to buy, and how to determine a color plan. If you have been building a fabric stash, you already have a selection of fabrics that represent your color sensibilities. Use these fabrics for Log Cabin landscapes and buildings, and add new purchases as needed. Look to stretch your existing palette in all directions: variety of color, scale of print, value range, style of pattern, and texture.

Shop for all-cotton fabrics at your favorite quilting shops, but don't overlook other sources. Remnant bins in home decorating fabric shops often turn up lightweight chintzes, polished

cottons, and silks that can bring luster and sheen to your work. The umbrellas in *A Day at the Beach* (page 5) are sewn from decorator cottons.

Shopping Strategy

To keep the palette interesting, purchase lots of fabrics in small amounts. If a quilt shop has fat quarters, check them out. Otherwise, ½-yard lengths are ample for cutting strips. One exception: Purchase enough border fabric yardage to allow uninterrupted lengthwise cuts, which will give straighter edges to your hanging quilts.

What About Prints?

Using different print styles and scales increases the visual texture of a quilt. Printed motifs don't have to be representational. As strips are cut, the motifs become randomly scattered. Flower and leaf designs are just as likely to end up on a roof or in the sky as in a meadow. Many times a print will simply lose its identity altogether when cut up and sewn alongside other fabrics.

How different prints interact with each other is more important than how they behave on their own. Value and pattern boundaries are relative to the quilt. A medium fabric in one palette may be the darkest value in another palette. A polka dot may go unnoticed in a palette of black and white graphic prints but become a lively accent elsewhere.

Hand-dyed batiks and mottled fabrics can offer diverse, dynamic movement, or they can play a supporting role. A blue-sky palette injected with streaks of hand-dyed pinks and corals can depict a brilliant sunset. In *A Day at the Beach* (page 5), hand-dyed and mottled fabrics hint at cloud formations. Printed fabrics varying in pattern scale and value give this sky a busy personality, consistent with the overall design.

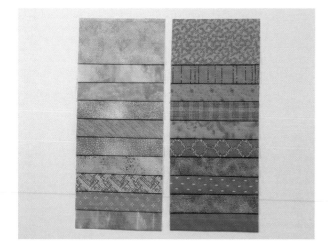

Lighter and darker blue fabrics for the sky in *Moms and Babes*. To ensure a "blue" sky, the lighter group of fabrics was used primarily for shorter logs.

Another way to use prints is by turning them over. The reverse side of a printed fabric is typically lighter than the face side, and often appears "frosted." In landscape quilts, the reverse side can effectively depict shadows, fallen snow, or distant scattered light. Some face side design motifs "shadow" through to the quilt top, offering subtle visual texture and automatic quilting lines.

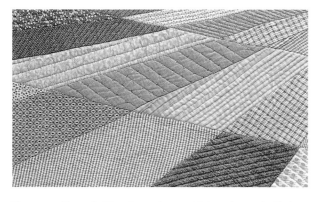

The reverse "frosted" sides of several green fabrics enhance the illusion of snow-dusted fields in *First Day of Winter*.

Plaids, Stripes, and Checks

Fabrics with strong linear patterns are always a challenge to work with. Quiltmakers have difficulty deciding where to use and how to cut these fabrics. Because plaids and stripes offer light and dark areas in the same cloth, they can work effectively in areas where depth is required. A light-colored plaid on a dark background can add

dimension to skyscrapers and clusters of buildings. Graphic grid patterns, especially high-contrast checks, are a perfect match for urban cityscapes. In architectural applications, plaids can fill in as windowpanes, door paneling, and roof shingles. In landscapes, stripes tend to work better than plaids, as long as you control the way a stripe is cut. Cutting parallel to the selvage is one way to keep plaids and stripes aligned.

USING COLOR

Traditional Log Cabin designs are built on color contrast. Within each block, the colors interact, yet remain distinct. When the blocks are joined together, dynamic, systematic patterns of light and dark flow across the entire quilt surface.

In Log Cabin landscapes, color plays a different role. Single colors flow from block to block to define large areas of the design. Only rarely do individual blocks enjoy the high-contrast role seen in traditional Log Cabin quilts. Instead, color changes separate mountains from sky, define fields, or erect houses. Subtle color changes characterize the face of a lamb, depict furrows in plowed ground, or hint at trees through the shadows.

When I made a formal study of color, I confess I found the color wheel lab exercises less than thrilling. The classes did, however, give me confidence to develop my own intuitive and emotional color sense. Color is a delightfully powerful and interactive part of my life. Color inspirations turn up constantly, and I respond to them spontaneously. Assuming that others want to enjoy the same sense of freedom, I hesitate to suggest *how* one should select colors. Instead, I encourage my students to embark on their own color journeys. Think of it as taking a vacation to a destination that really interests you. The journey begins the day we first assess the fabrics you bring to class. Devising a value scale within a limited palette forces you to think about and study your colors. Once you select the palette, making a few sample blocks gives you an opportunity to see the color movement, relationships, and contrasts. Each quilt you make becomes a unique color experiment, with new avenues to explore.

When Colors Meld Together

In many landscape quilt designs, the color is limited to just a few color families. There might be green meadows, gray mountains, and a blue sky. The overall palette is soft and "cooperative," with just enough color tension to keep the design interesting. Here it's especially important to mix in different prints, scales, and textures to ensure variety within each color family. Choose fabrics not for their beauty, but for how they project and work together in the quilt.

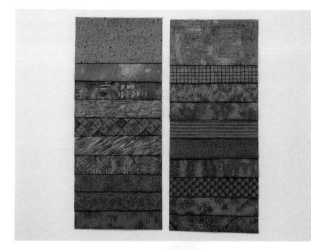

An assortment of muted greens for the pasture in *Moms and Babes*

Instead of choosing just one or two muted green fabrics for a meadow, audition two or three dozen. A collection of green fabrics selected to work as "one" meadow doesn't have to be limited to a single dye lot or pattern scale. In fact, the ideal fabrics will differentiate themselves somewhat, so that individual logs are discernable. This creates gentle, subtle movement in the quilt, without resorting to disruptive color contrasts. A successful landscape will use literally dozens of fabrics, some slightly darker and some slightly lighter than the core palette, for each area. An added advantage to working with a multitude of

fabrics is that you are less likely to run out before the piecing is complete.

Use It Up

Ugly fabrics cut up nicely for Log Cabins, so don't be afraid to clean out your stash. When they are cut into 1" strips and sewn into ½"-wide finished logs, even you will wonder where those fabric dogs have gone!

When Colors Contrast

Key shapes and motifs are made more visible by color contrast. In *Morning Graze* (page 6), soft greens act as a neutral backdrop to set off the white sheep and lambs. In *Up at Sunrise* (page 56), the bright primary colors in the balloon show off nicely against a bright green turf. Yellow and orange suns showcase brilliantly against blue skies.

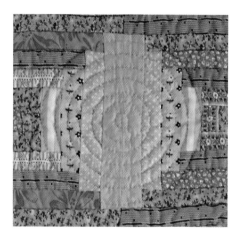

Sun in *Seascape*

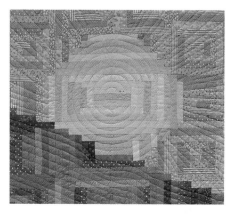

Sun in *Daybreak*

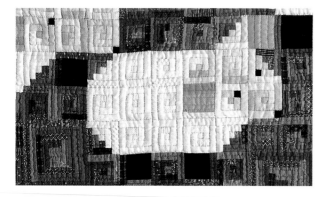

White, off-white, black, and pink fabrics make a lamb for *Morning Graze.*

Color changes within or across blocks can further define image. The lambs in *Morning Graze* are made of 2½" x 2½" squares. These small, easy-to-sew blocks are arranged side by side. No ingenious designing was necessary. The body and facial features are effective because of the color choices and placement. Black cornerstones become the eyes and nose, and pink strips become ears. When images contain multiple colors, the background color requires extra consideration. Choose a background palette for adequate contrast, making sure that the background doesn't overpower key images.

Color in Buildings

When blocks make up houses or buildings, the color can become more playful. In many house quilt designs, such as *Row Houses* (page 78), the underlying block pattern is simple and repetitive, but color introduces an element of serendipity. One house is colorful and bright, while an adjacent house is understated and neutral. How the different fabrics work in relation to each other is key when you plan the palette. A successful interplay is influenced as much by the neutrals as by the brights and bolds. Neutrals act as stabilizers for more intense colors, and keep a quilt interesting without being visually demanding. Changes in fabric texture, sheen, and pattern also contribute in understated ways.

Color changes in *Row Houses*

Homes along a canal in Burano, Italy, provide color inspiration for a future quilt.

Coloring for Depth

A key goal of a Log Cabin landscape is to convey a sense of space and perspective. Different colors and values help signal changes in depth, cueing the eye to see trees, fields, mountains, and other elements of the scene as nearby, distant, or somewhere in between.

Typically, images in the foreground are brighter and sharper, while distant features are more subdued, with less color definition between shapes. *Canterbury Fields* (page 101) provides a useful example. In the foreground, greens, oranges, and browns create a crisp patchwork of fields. The distant mountains are pieced from grays, with whites thrown in for the snowcapped peaks. The relatively close values of the grays enhance the illusion that the mountains are miles away. Within this tight gray palette, assorted prints give each mountain a distinct identity. The prints keep the scene lively and interesting when the quilt is viewed up close.

Another way to convey three-dimensional space is to superimpose one object on top of another. This is especially effective with houses and buildings, but it also works with trees, rock outcroppings, rivers, and other natural forms. The eye reads the shapes on top as being closer. Make those shapes lighter or brighter in color to carry through the illusion. Conversely, make the "underneath" shapes duller or neutral in tone. *Sustainable* (page 47) uses this principle to create the tree shadows.

Centuries-old streets and stairways in Girona, Spain, present challenging three-dimensional scenes for the quilter to interpret. In this view, a light-colored mansion is a distant focal point, and the middle ground is enveloped in shadows.

Quilt Assembly

MAKING BLOCKS

There are several ways to make Log Cabin blocks. The projects in this book use logs that are precut to the exact dimensions required for each block. The precut logs are organized into piles and then stitched together following a predetermined piecing route. This method promotes accuracy, yet still allows color spontaneity. You'll find you make efficient use of your cutting and sewing time as well as your fabrics.

Cutting the Logs

Press the fabrics for your quilt. Stack only as many layers as you can comfortably and accurately cut with your rotary cutter. For me, this is generally two layers (because I cut sitting down) and never more than four layers. Cut the fabrics into strips, and then cut the strips into shorter logs. Refer to the log cutting guides in the project's instructions for the width and length of each log.

> **Cutting Guide Tip**
> Tape a copy of the log cutting guide to your rotary cutting ruler for handy reference as you cut.

I like to cut strips for Log Cabin piecing on the lengthwise grain of the fabric, or parallel to the selvage. I find that the warp threads run truer than the woof threads, giving me strips that are consistently straighter and that have less stretch than those cut on the crosswise grain. I make an exception for stripes and other patterns that I want to feature on the crosswise grain. Fat quarters and ½-yard cuts provide 18" of fabric—a length I can comfortably reach with one pass of my rotary cutter.

When you are combining dozens of different fabrics from one color family, cut no more than two or three strips from each fabric, or the amount you'll be using right away. Never "strip" an entire piece of fabric in one session, as you don't know what log widths will be needed in the future.

As you cut the logs, sort and stack them by size and color family. I do all my cutting, sorting, and labeling at the cutting table. I don't sit down at the sewing machine until the blocks are ready to construct. Separating the tasks in this way helps my concentration. It lets me use 120 or more different fabrics without feeling completely overwhelmed by the prospect!

> **On Your Own**
> When you design a block, make a log cutting guide to go with it. Draw the block at actual size on graph paper. Label the logs A, B, C, and so forth. Write down the dimensions of each log. Now add ½" to each dimension to determine the cut log size.

Before: Cut logs are arranged in size order. The blue-gray logs on the right feature assorted fabrics.

After: A finished traditional Log Cabin block.

Be sure to follow the block diagram and alphabetical piecing order carefully, as each block is a little different. In Courthouse Steps blocks, the logs are added in pairs. Elongated blocks may have two or three A's joined at the center. In blocks with Log A cornerstones, join all the cornerstones to their respective logs first, and proceed alphabetically from there.

The Piecing Route

The letters assigned to each log determine the piecing route: A, B, C, and so forth. To begin, place Log A and Log B face sides together and stitch along one edge, using a ¼" seam. Finger-press the seam allowance toward B. Stitch Log C to the AB unit, referring to the block diagram for the proper position. Finger-press the seam allowance toward C. Continue adding the logs in alphabetical order (following the numbered steps), finger-pressing after each addition, until the block is complete.

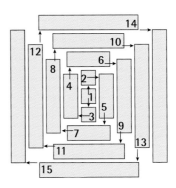

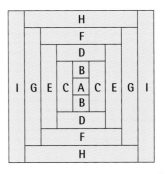

Courthouse Steps Piecing Route

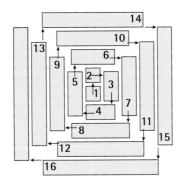

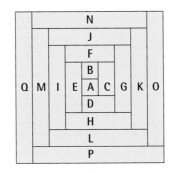

Traditional Block Piecing Route

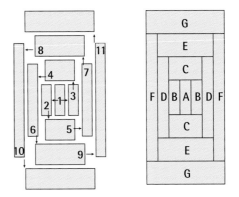

Elongated Block Piecing Route

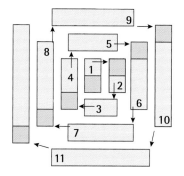

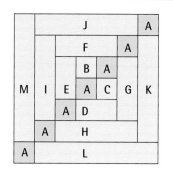

Cornerstones Block Piecing Route

If the quilt design uses lots of identical blocks, sew them assembly-line style. First sew all the A's and B's, then join all the C's to the AB's, and so on. Cutting many logs at once and sorting them by length makes it easy to mix up different fabrics within a color family or value. A sky made up of 40 rectangular blocks can be sewn directly from your log stacks without the need for individual block number assignments. If there is ever a time for chain piecing, this is it! Any set of identical blocks can be chain-pieced—even if they ultimately end up in totally different areas of the quilt.

Checking for Accuracy

Precut logs give you a built-in way to check the accuracy of the block in progress. Each new log you add should fit exactly. If it doesn't, check the accuracy of the previous seam allowances. Even with an accurate presser foot or gauge, sewing a ¼" seam isn't automatically guaranteed. As in driving a car, you have to watch and be alert at all times. In my classes, students using demonstration-model sewing machines often have the machines set properly but misgauge the alignment of the fabric, consistently sewing seams too narrow or too wide. Other mistakes include stitching the wrong log to a block, piecing out of sequence, or stretching a long, narrow log. Any of these mistakes can affect the way a block comes together.

Off-center blocks can be especially tricky, starting off in one direction and then changing course. Keep in mind that rectangular and off-center blocks, unlike traditional square blocks, cannot be turned around to get the mirror image; you have to use a different piecing route to make them.

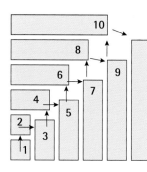
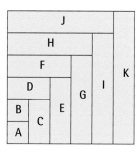

Off-Center Block Piecing Route

¼" Seam Allowance

The most important attachment I have on my sewing machine is a ¼" presser foot designed especially for patchwork. Some machines adjust the needle position for a ¼" seam. Another option is to affix masking tape to the machine's throat plate exactly ¼" to the right of the needle. When you sew, use the edge of the tape as a guide for the raw edge of the fabric.

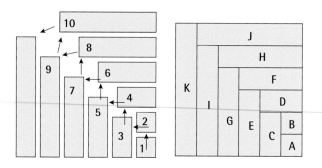

Piecing the Mirror-Image Block

Once you've made a block, double-check it against the quilt diagram. Make sure that the log colors fall in the right places, and that the block orientation is correct. Write the block number on a self-stick reusable label and affix it to the finished block. Mark a small arrow on the label to tell you which edge of the block is the top.

JOINING THE BLOCKS

When you've completed all the Log Cabin blocks, lay them out in numbered order, following the quilt diagram. Recheck the blocks one by one. Here's your chance to find maverick blocks that are positioned upside down or sideways. View the arrangement through a reducing glass to evaluate the overall image. Is the original design concept coming through? Make any needed corrections, including redesigning and resewing any blocks, if necessary.

When you are satisfied with the layout, stitch the blocks together one row at time, using a ¼" seam allowance. In each row, press all the seam allowances in one direction. Alternate this direction from row to row so that the seams will butt when the rows are joined together. Stitch the rows together, pinning if required. Press all of the row seam allowances in the same direction. When blocks are arranged on point, stitch them together in diagonal rows, adding a setting triangle at each end.

The Reducing Glass

An apartment door peephole, sold at hardware stores, makes an inexpensive reducing glass. Use it to assess scale drawings, fabric palettes, and quilt block layouts.

MAKING BORDERS

A good border emphasizes the quilt blocks without stealing attention from them. A border acts much like a picture frame, lending structure, interest, and thematic continuity to the quilt. Not all quilts need a border, but if you do add one, be sure to give it a role besides simply making the quilt larger.

There are several border options to consider. Which one you choose depends on the quilt. Plain border strips offer visual relief from a busy quilt. Multistrip borders with mitered corners accentuate the framed effect. An inner border can act as a spacer between the quilt and a pieced border, setting off both of them.

A border can repeat colors, fabrics, and patterns that appear in the Log Cabin blocks, or it may introduce new fabrics. Narrow strips of fabric left over from the Log Cabin blocks can be incorporated into the border for color continuity. In *Hemlocks* (page 110), the leftover strips are joined end to end, adding subtle dimension as the colors move between dark and bright. Little patchwork blocks lined up in a border take on a life of their own and keep your eye circulating around the quilt.

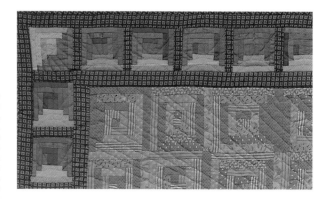

Sun blocks form a thematic border in *Daybreak*.

Mountains and Meadows (page 108), one of my earliest Log Cabin landscapes, features a square-within-a-square border sewn from high-contrast fabrics. The lighter fabric doesn't appear at all within the quilt, yet still works effectively to frame it. Occasionally, a focus fabric will inspire the color scheme for a group of blocks without actually appearing in them. The outer border surrounding the paint chips in *Carolina Row* (below and page 88) is such an example. Like a grand finale, this colorful decorator fabric doesn't make its appearance until the very end.

Carolina Row's focus fabric appears only in the outer border.

Cutting Border Strips

When I make Log Cabin blocks, I precut the strips. With borders, I wait until after the blocks are joined before doing any cutting. Then I measure the actual width and length of the quilt top, horizontally and vertically through the middle, to calculate the precise border dimensions required. The project directions tell what width to cut the border strips. The length, when given, is approximate. You'll determine the actual length to cut when your quilt is in progress.

I prefer to cut long, continuous border strips on the lengthwise grain of the fabric. This takes additional yardage but results in a sturdy border with minimal stretch. The yardage listed for each project allows for these seam-free lengthwise cuts. If a fabric will be used for both the blocks and the border, cut and set aside a length for the borders

at the beginning. Then cut the remainder on the crosswise grain into ½-yard lengths and proceed from there to the stripping.

Striped Borders

A cross-grain cut is the only way to achieve certain striped effects in the border. Look for striped decorator cottons, which stretch less on the cross-grain than quilting cottons.

Butting the Corners

Square and rectangular Log Cabin blocks have butted corners, meaning one log is joined to another log at a 90° angle. Butting the border strips is a way of extending the Log Cabin construction beyond the blocks, adding to the unity of the quilt. The strip widths can vary or they can match.

Cut the top and bottom border strips. The length should be the same as the horizontal measurement of the quilt top. Join the strips to the quilt, using a ¼" seam allowance. Press each seam allowance toward the border.

Remeasure the quilt through the vertical center, including the top and bottom border strips. Cut the side border strips to this length, join them to the quilt top, and press. Repeat the entire process for each additional border, measuring the quilt with the attached border horizontally before cutting the top and bottom borders, and so forth.

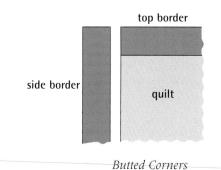

Butted Corners

Mitering the Corners

Mitered corners have a diagonal seam. In this corner treatment, all four border strips are cut at the same time and must be the same width. Cut the top and bottom border strips equal to the horizontal measurement of the quilt top plus twice the border width, plus 5" (for extra allowance). Cut the side border strips equal to the vertical measurement of the quilt top plus twice the border width, plus 5". Note that in a square quilt, all four border strips will be the same length.

Center one strip on the appropriate edge of the quilt, face sides together and raw edges matching. Pin from the center out, letting the strip extend evenly beyond the edge of the quilt top at each end. Stitch in place, using a ¼" seam allowance; start and stop the stitching line ¼" from each end. Press the seam allowance toward the border. Join the remaining three strips to the quilt top in the same way.

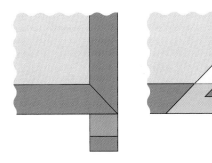

Making the 45° Fold   *Squaring Up*

Bring the long edges of the border strips face sides together and fold the entire quilt top in half diagonally. Pin along the pressed-in crease. Stitch along the crease line from the inside corner to the outside corner, backstitching at each end. Be careful not to stretch the fabric. Trim off the excess border strips ¼" beyond the stitching. Press the seam open. Repeat to miter all four corners.

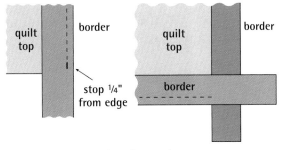

Sewing the Borders

Stitching the Miter

Lay the quilt top face up on a flat surface. Start at any corner. Let one border overlap the other border at a right angle. Fold the top border under itself at a 45° angle. Double-check the corner with a drafting triangle or a rotary cutting grid ruler to make sure the corner is square. Press to set the crease.

Multiple Borders

Multiple borders are made by sewing several strips of fabric together. Each border is constructed separately, then joined to the quilt as a unit. This technique is especially useful for matching the stripes in mitered corners.

QUILTING AND FINISHING

There are various ways to finish a quilt—and dozens of materials, tools, classes, magazines, and books to help you do it. If the array of battings, threads, needles, and thimbles available to quilters makes you feel perpetually confused, you're not alone. Watch others demonstrate tools and techniques, and then experiment with products that interest you. Look for quilting and finishing methods that suit your needs and personality.

Layering the Quilt

Choose a batting depending on whether you plan to quilt by hand or by machine. I quilt by hand, so I haven't experimented widely in this area. My choice is Fairfield's Traditional, a 100% polyester batting. This bonded batting helps a quilt lie flat against the wall—important in large wall quilts that hang for months at a time. It doesn't needle as well as some other polyester battings, but its sturdiness and smooth drape are compensation enough for me. I switch to Fairfield's Cotton Classic (80% cotton/20% polyester) when a quilt has a black backing and extensively dark patchwork. This batting doesn't beard through the dark fabrics as readily as an all-polyester batting does. Bearding tends to be a problem in quilts that get heavy use.

I usually cut the batting 2" to 3" larger than the quilt top. If the quilt top is small, I tape the backing to a countertop and pin the layers together. After basting along the outer edge, I do some overall basting before securing the sandwich in a round hoop for hand quilting.

For larger quilts, I secure the backing and batting in a large, fully extended quilt frame. I stretch the quilt top over the frame and pin and baste the layers together, starting at the outside edge and working my way in. I hand-quilt in the same manner. Once I have sufficient quilting around the border, I begin rolling the quilt inward. I find that if I can stitch some basic quilting lines every 10" to 12", basting the interior of the quilt isn't necessary. I remove the quilt from the frame and finish the quilting in a round hoop. Making the project portable increases the likelihood of my completing it.

I mark designs like animal tracks, leaves, and concentric circles on the surface as needed. But striped and printed fabrics often provide enough pattern to guide the quilting without marking. Random lines and curves are easy to stitch freehand, as are blocks quilted near the ditch of the seam.

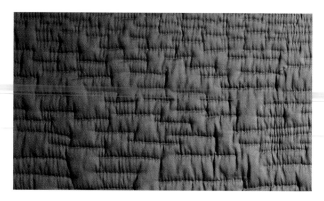

Random lines depict calm water on the reverse side of *Sailor's Delight.*

Quilting as Design

Quilting stitches tie the fabrics together, literally and figuratively. Quilting is a utilitarian necessity, but it also contributes to the overall design. It can define areas or shapes, unify thematic elements, and add movement. Quilting plays a more significant role in my Log Cabin images than in the other types of quilt work that I do. I've seen quilting stitches transform a quilt top time and again.

What quilting can do:

■ **Emphasize individual logs.** Quilt in or near the ditch for this effect.

■ **Lead your eye** into the center of the quilt, or toward a featured area.

■ **Feature special motifs.** Animal tracks on land, fish in the water, and stands of pine trees are examples of quilted motifs that can cross block and log boundaries. As the overall scene becomes stronger, individual blocks diminish in importance.

■ **Add landscaping contours.** Echo quilting can emphasize mountains, valleys, and plains, and can bring character and form to images that the fabric transitions only hint at.

■ **Create perspective in waterscapes.** In *Sailors' Delight* (page 109), broken, widely spaced horizontal lines in the foreground depict an area close to shore. As the water moves out toward the horizon, the quilting lines become shorter and denser.

■ **Soften a sky.** The blocky lines of a Log Cabin sky are softened when the quilting lines meander across the surface. This technique is especially effective when the logs are cut from many different blues.

■ **Rev up a sky.** The sky intensifies when quilted sunrays radiate straight through the patchwork logs.

Powerful quilting lines radiate out from the sun in *A Day at the Beach*.

Binding the Quilt

There are several methods for binding a quilt. I prefer the strength and thickness of a double-fold bias binding, especially on a bed quilt. The bias cut provides flexibility when turning the corners.

To make the binding, start with a large, well-pressed square of fabric, up to 44" x 44". The binding fabric can match the outer border or the backing, or it can contrast, for an added mini border. Striped fabric cut on the bias is especially effective. Fold the square on the diagonal, from corner to corner, to find the true bias. Then rotary-cut strips parallel to the diagonal fold, 2 to 2½" wide, until you have enough strips to go around the perimeter of your quilt. Cut off the selvages and stitch the strips together, end to end, making diagonal seams. Press the seams open. Fold the binding in half lengthwise, face side out and raw edges matching, and press. Trim off the ears.

To attach the binding, align both raw edges on the edge of the quilt top. Starting a few inches from one end, stitch ¼" from the edge all around through all the layers. Pivot and turn at the corners, cutting into the binding seam allowance to provide ease. When you near the starting point, stop. Sew the loose ends together with a diagonal seam, trim off the excess, and press the seam open. Stitch the joined section to the quilt top. Trim the excess batting and backing even with the raw edges. Turn the folded edge of the binding onto the back of the quilt and blind-stitch in place.

For more information on other block and quilt assembly techniques, including foundation piecing, that can be adapted to Log Cabin landscapes, see For Further Reading (page 111).

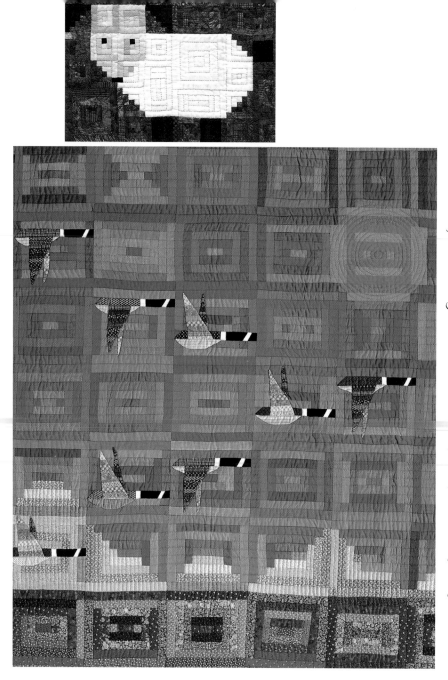

Put your block knowledge and fabric stash to work as you re-create these nine Log cabin originals. Each project uses log cutting guides, lots of colorful block illustrations, and step-by-step directions. Follow the quilt diagrams to lay out your completed blocks and bring these exciting Log cabin landscapes to life.

Quilts
to Make

Part 2

Sustainable

Sustainable, 75½" x 43½", 1999.
Machine-pieced, hand-quilted. Cottons, polyester batting.

The numerous tree quilts I've designed reflect my husband Glenn's career in forestry, and my growing up with parents who practiced stewardship of the land. My siblings and I strive to sustain the land we inherited from our parents. The quilt *Sustainable* is a direct tribute to these influences in my life. Sustainable forestry is the management of all forest resources in a way that fulfills present-day needs, while also ensuring that resources are available for future generations. This wall quilt's simple pine trees symbolize today's forest. The tree shadows represent forests of the future—the sustained production of a renewable resource. I used some tree fabrics wrong side up in the shadow areas, symbolizing the connection between today and the future.

Sizes at a Glance

QUILT: 75½" x 43½"
BLOCK 1: 3½" x 7"
BLOCK 2: 4¾" x 7"
BLOCK 3: 4½" x 7"
BLOCK 4: 4¾" x 7"

Plantation of young loblolly pines

MATERIALS

trees, border squares	■	1⅝ yards total assorted greens
snow, border squares	□	2⅛ yards total assorted whites
tree shadows	▨	1 yard total assorted light medium greens, including reverse side of tree fabrics
tree trunks	■	⅓ yard total assorted dark grays
tree trunk shadows	▨	⅓ yard total assorted medium grays, including reverse side of tree trunk fabrics
borders, bias binding		2⅛ yards white-on-white stripe
batting		79" x 48"
backing		2¾ yards

Fabric notes: The shadow fabrics should be slightly lighter than the tree and trunk fabrics. Sometimes you can use the reverse side of a tree or trunk fabric. Audition the reverse side alongside your other selected shadow palettes (medium to light greens for the trees, and medium grays for the trunks) to see if they are compatible. Some reverse sides have a frosted appearance and may be too light. Don't use a reverse side unless it harmonizes with the other shadow fabrics.

MAKING THE BLOCKS

For general instructions, see Elongated Courthouse Steps Block (page 27) and Making Blocks (page 38). Be sure to follow each log cutting guide and block diagram exactly. To maintain the correct log and color orientation, sort and label the pieces as you work. Make 92 blocks total.

SUSTAINABLE BLOCK 1 LOG CUTTING GUIDE			
Log	Cut	Width	Length
A	2	1¼"	1½"
B	2	1½"	2"
C	2	1"	3½"
D	2	1½"	3"
E	2	1"	5½"
F	2	1½"	4"

Finished Block Size: 3½" x 7"

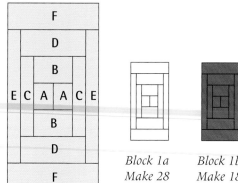

Block 1

Block 1a Make 28

Block 1b Make 18

Block 1c Make 5

Block 1d Make 3

Block 1e Make 6

Block 1f Make 2

Block 1g Make 2

Block 1h Make 10

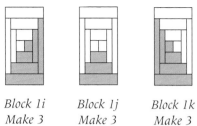

Block 1i
Make 3

Block 1j
Make 3

Block 1k
Make 3

SUSTAINABLE BLOCK 3 LOG CUTTING GUIDE

Log	Cut	Width	Length
A	2	1¼"	1½"
B	2	1½"	2"
C	2	1"	3½"
D	2	1½"	3"
E	2	1"	5½"
F	2	1½"	4"
G	2	1"	7½"

Finished Block Size: 4½" x 7"

SUSTAINABLE BLOCK 2 LOG CUTTING GUIDE

Log	Cut	Width	Length
A	2	1¼"	1½"
B	2	1½"	2"
C	2	1"	3½"
D	2	1½"	3"
E	2	1"	5½"
F	2	1½"	4"
G	1	1"	7½"
G+	1	1¼"	7½"

Finished Block Size: 4¾" x 7"

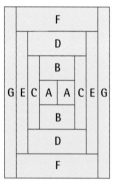

Block 3

Block 3
Make 3

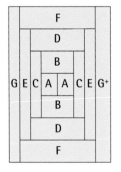

Block 2

Block 2
Make 3

Fabric Key

- greens
- whites
- light medium greens
- dark grays
- medium grays

SUSTAINABLE BLOCK 4 LOG CUTTING GUIDE			
Log	Cut	Width	Length
A	2	1¼"	1½"
B	2	1½"	2"
C	2	1"	3½"
D	2	1½"	3"
E	2	1"	5½"
F	2	1½"	4"
G	1	1"	7½"
G+	1	1¼"	7½"

Finished Block Size: 4¾" x 7"

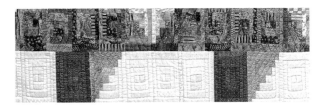

Detail of *Sustainable* tree trunks

3. Follow the Border Cutting Guide to cut the middle border strips only. (The remaining strips will be cut later.) Stitch the assorted green and white strips together in pairs. Press toward the darker fabric. Cut each strip set into 12 segments 1½" wide, for 216 segments total. Join 68 assorted segments in a checked pattern for the top and bottom middle borders, and 40 assorted segments for each side middle border. Press.

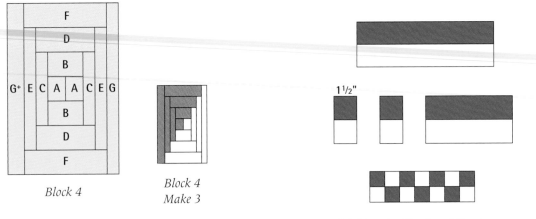

Making the Checkered Borders

Block 4

*Block 4
Make 3*

ASSEMBLING THE QUILT

For general instructions, see Joining the Blocks (page 41), Making Borders (page 41), and Quilting and Finishing (page 44).

1. Lay out 92 rectangular blocks, referring to the quilt photograph (page 47) and quilt diagram (page 51). Rows 1–4 have 19 blocks each. Row 5 has 16 blocks. Make sure each tree trunk is centered under a tree. Step back and squint, or use a reducing glass, to search for maverick blocks—blocks that are upside down or incorrectly pieced. Revise as needed.

2. Stitch the blocks together in rows. Press. Join the rows. Press.

4. Measure the quilt top and the middle border. Double-check the measurements in the Border Cutting Guide: Recalculate the width and length of the inner border strips, if necessary, so that the checkered borders will come together exactly. Cut the inner border strips on the lengthwise grain. Cut the outer border strips crosswise.

SUSTAINABLE BORDER CUTTING GUIDE				
Border	Fabric	Cut	Width	Length
top/bottom inner	white-on-white	2	1"*	72"*
side inner	white-on-white	2	1¼"*	72"*
middle	assorted greens	18	1½"	18"
middle	assorted whites	18	1½"	18"
outer	white-on-white	7	2"	36"

*measurement is approximate

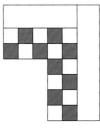

Border Corner Detail

5. Sew the top and bottom inner borders to the quilt top. Press. Join the side inner borders to the quilt top. Press. Add the middle borders in the same order, pressing after each addition.

6. Sew the outer border strips into one long strip. Measure the quilt top to determine the length of the outer borders. Cut the top and bottom outer borders from the long strip. Sew them to the quilt top. Press. Add the side outer borders in the same way. Press.

7. Layer and finish the quilt. Quilt closely spaced parallel lines inside the trees, the tree trunks, and their shadows. Bind the edges of the quilt with a 2¼"-wide bias strip cut from a 26" x 26" square of the same striped fabric you used in the border (see Binding the Quilt, page 45).

Sustainable Quilting Design

Row 1	1a	1a	1a	1a	1a	1j	1a	1a	1a	1a	1a	1j	1a	1a	1a	1a	1a	1j	1a
Row 2	1a	1a	1c	1d	1i	1h	1k	1a	1c	1d	1i	1h	1k	1a	1c	1d	1i	1h	1k
Row 3	1a	1c	1b	1b	1e	1h	1h	1g	1b	1b	1e	1h	1h	1g	1b	1b	1e	1h	1h
Row 4	1c	1b	1b	1b	1b	1e	1f	1b	1b	1b	1b	1e	1f	1b	1b	1b	1b	1e	1h
Row 5	1a	2	3	4	1a	1a	2	3	4	1a	1a	2	3	4	1a	1a

Quilt Diagram

Mainely Pines

Mainely Pines, 25" x 25", 2002.
Machine-pieced, hand-quilted. Cottons, polyester batting.

When the Pine Tree Quilters Guild, Incorporated, of Maine invited me to design a small quilt for their charity auction, I took my inspiration from the guild name. To meet the size limitation set by the guild, I used ½"-wide finished logs in 2½" x 2½" Log Cabin blocks. A diagonal setting turned these tiny blocks into pine trees, with cornerstones acting as tree trunks. Since each block takes only two rounds, the trees were somewhat sparse. By "borrowing" the last log in two adjacent blocks, I was able to gain two additional branches per tree.

I made the setting triangles around the edges of the quilt by cutting square Log Cabin blocks in half on the diagonal. Blocks for setting triangles are usually made ½" larger than the interior blocks to allow for precise block points at the quilt edges. In *Mainely Pines,* I used the same block size throughout, so that the border strips cut in on the pieced blocks. Still, this method saves time and makes frugal use of fabrics.

Sizes
at a Glance

QUILT: 25" x 25"
BLOCK: 2½" x 2½"

MATERIALS

trees		⅓ yard total assorted dark greens
tree trunks		⅛ yard dark brown
grass		⅝ yard total assorted muted greens
sky		½ yard total assorted light blues
sun		⅛ yard total assorted bright yellows
borders, bias binding		1 yard dark striped
batting		28" x 28"
backing		¾ yard

MAINELY PINES BLOCK 1 LOG CUTTING GUIDE			
Log	Cut	Width	Length
A	3	1"	1"
B	1	1"	1"
C	1	1"	1"
D	1	1"	1½"
E	1	1"	2"
F	1	1"	2"
G	1	1"	2"
H	1	1"	2½"
I	1	1"	3"

Finished Block Size: 2½" x 2½"

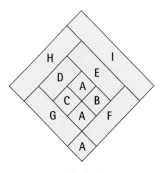

Block 1

MAKING THE BLOCKS

For general instructions, see Traditional Log Cabin Block (page 22), Cornerstones Log Cabin Block (page 25), and Making Blocks (page 38). Follow the log cutting guides and block diagrams to make 75 blocks total. Sort and label the pieces as you work.

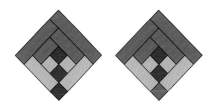

Block 1a
Make 11

Block 1b
Make 1

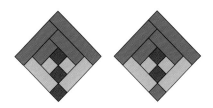

Block 1c
Make 3

Block 1d
Make 1

MAINELY PINES BLOCK 2 LOG CUTTING GUIDE			
Log	Cut	Width	Length
A	1	1"	1"
B	1	1"	1"
C	1	1"	1½"
D	1	1"	1½"
E	1	1"	2"
F	1	1"	2"
G	1	1"	2½"
H	1	1"	2½"
I	1	1"	3"

Finished Block Size: 2½" x 2½"

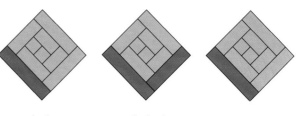

Block 2g
Make 7

Block 2h
Make 1

Block 2i
Make 2

MAINELY PINES BLOCK 3 LOG CUTTING GUIDE			
Log	Cut	Width	Length
A	1	1"	1"
B	1	1"	1"
C	1	1"	1½"
D	1	1"	1½"
E	1	1"	2"
F	1	1"	2"
G	1	1"	2½"
H	1	1"	2½"
I	1	1"	1"
J	1	1"	2½"

Finished Block Size: 2½" x 2½"

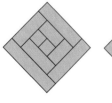

Block 2

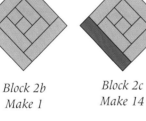

Block 3

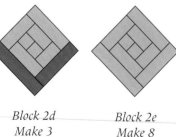

Block 2a
Make 8

Block 2b
Make 1

Block 2c
Make 14

Block 2d
Make 3

Block 2e
Make 8

Block 2f
Make 1

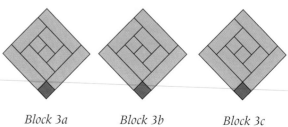

Block 3a
Make 7

Block 3b
Make 1

Block 3c
Make 6

ASSEMBLING THE QUILT

For general instructions, see Joining the Blocks (page 41), Making Borders (page 41), and Quilting and Finishing (page 44).

1. Lay out 60 whole blocks on point, referring to the quilt photograph (page 52) and quilt diagram.

2. Audition the remaining 15 blocks to fill in the edges. Referring to the photograph on page 62, use a rotary cutter and ruler to cut each of the 15 blocks in half, corner to corner, to make 24 setting triangles (plus 6 triangles left over). Arrange the triangles around the whole blocks.

3. Stitch the blocks and triangles together in diagonal rows. Press. Join the rows together. Press.

4. Measure the quilt top to determine the lengths of the border strips. From the dark striped fabric, cut four 2¼"-wide border strips on the crosswise grain. Sew the top and bottom border strips to the quilt top. Press. Join the side borders to the quilt top. Press.

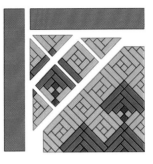

Border Corner Detail

5. Layer and finish the quilt. Quilt the sun with semicircular lines, and use straight lines to show the sunshine radiating across the sky. Quilt the grass logs near the ditch of each seam to create highlights and shadows. Leave the trees puffy; quilt only around the outer edge and to define the logs that form the trunk at the vertical center of each tree. Quilt the border in a repetitive crossbar style that accentuates the stripes. Bind the edges with a 2⅛"-wide bias strip cut from an 18" x 18" square of the same striped fabric you used in the border (see Binding the Quilt, page 45).

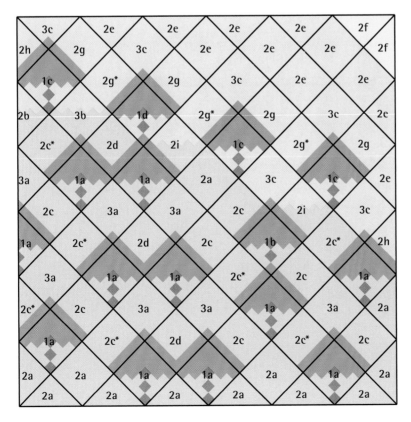

Fabric Key

- dark greens
- dark brown
- muted greens
- light blues
- bright yellows

* Rotate completed block when placing

Quilt Diagram

Up at Sunrise

Up at Sunrise, 73½" x 77¼", 2002.
Machine-pieced, hand-quilted. Cottons, polyester batting.

S pain's flat, fertile, southeastern coastal plain is a striking landscape dominated by orange groves, vegetable farms, and rice
paddies. The region is known as the Levante, which means east,
because of the way the sun rises out of the Mediterranean Sea.
Turn your back to the sea and you face arid mountains dotted with
olive groves. The lush, irrigated pastures in between are dotted
with sheep. Deeply inspired, I drew an aerial view of a colorful hot
air balloon floating above the vista. Randomly placed yellow cornerstones depict buttercups
in the green meadow.
Stylized trees against freshly
plowed ground represent
a young olive grove. The
balloon's strong colors are
counterbalanced by colored
bars in the middle border.

Farmland in Spain's Levante region in southern Catalonia

Sizes
at a Glance

QUILT: 73½" x 77¼"
BLOCK 1: 5¼" x 5¼"
BLOCK 2: 5¼" x 5¼"
BLOCK 3: 5¼" x 5¼"
BLOCK 4: 5¾" x 5¾"
BLOCK 5: 5¾" x 5¾"
BLOCK 6: 4" x 4"

MATERIALS

sky		1 yard assorted light blues
balloon, border color bars		⅜ yard assorted yellows
		⅜ yard assorted oranges
		⅜ yard assorted purples
		⅜ yard assorted reds
		¾ yard assorted royal blues
gondola		1 fat quarter light print
ropes (cornerstones)		⅛ yard black or darks
artichoke fields		½ yard total assorted muted greens
asparagus patch, border color bars		⅔ yard assorted spring greens
plowed ground		½ yard assorted browns
wheat stubble		⅔ yard assorted golds and deep yellows
meadow with buttercups		1¼ yards assorted medium greens
buttercups (cornerstones)		⅛ yard yellow floral
olive grove ground		1 yard assorted light browns and tans
olive trees		⅝ yard assorted dark greens
tree trunks		⅛ yard dark brown
sea		¾ yard assorted aqua blues
inner and outer borders, backing		7 yards navy
batting		77" x 81"
bias binding		⅞ yard

MAKING THE BLOCKS

For general instructions, see Traditional Log Cabin Block (page 22), Offset Center Variation Block (page 24), Cornerstones Log Cabin Block (page 25), and Making Blocks (page 38). The White House Steps variation (page 22) is used for the brightly colored blocks in the balloon. Blocks 4 and 5 are constructed ½" larger than the interior blocks. During the quilt assembly, blocks 4 and 5 will be cut in half, corner to corner, to make setting triangles. Make 160 blocks total.

Up at Sunrise Block 1 Log Cutting Guide

Log	Cut	Width	Length
A	1	1¼"	1¼"
B	1	1¼"	1¼"
C	1	1¼"	2"
D	1	1¼"	2"
E	1	1¼"	2¾"
F	1	1¼"	2¾"
G	1	1¼"	3½"
H	1	1¼"	3½"
I	1	1¼"	4¼"
J	1	1¼"	4 ¼"
K	1	1¼"	5"
L	1	1¼"	5"
M	1	1¼"	5¾"

Finished Block Size: 5¼" x 5¼"

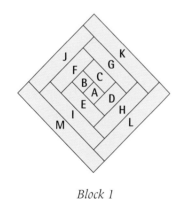

Block 1

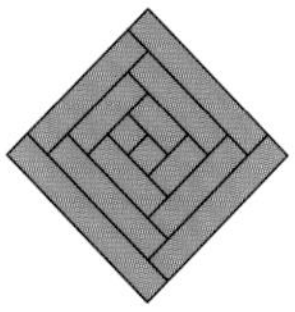

Block 1a
Make 12

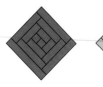

Block 1b
Make 3

Block 1c
Make 8

Block 1d
Make 10

Block 1e
Make 6

Block 1f
Make 9

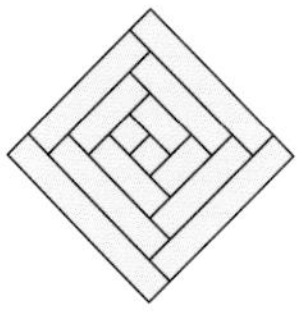

Block 1g
Make 4

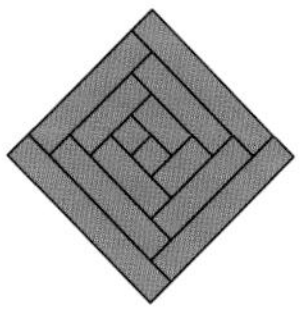

Block 1h
Make 4

Block 1i
Make 3

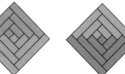

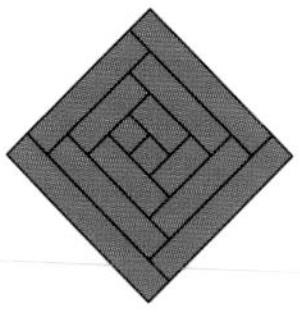

Block 1j
Make 4

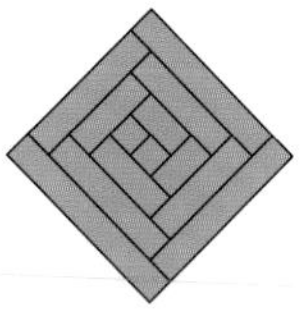

Block 1k
Make 10

Block 1l Make 14
Add buttercup
cornerstones
(1¼" x 1¼")

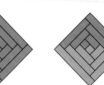

Block 1m
Make 4

Block 1n
Make 3

Block 1o
Make 2

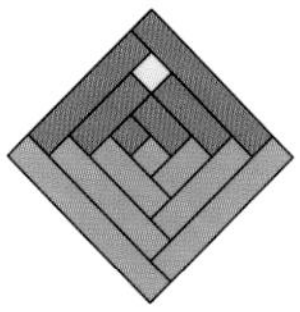

Block 1p
Make 5
Add buttercup
cornerstones
(1¼" x 1¼")

Block 1q
Make 3

Block 1r
Make 3

Adding Buttercups

Cut 32 yellow floral 1¼" x 1¼" cornerstones for the buttercups. Substitute buttercup cornerstones for 8 of the A or B logs in the Block 1l log stacks. Cut 2 or 3 each of the Block 1l (logs C through M) and the Block 1p logs C, F, G, J, and K ¾" shorter than needed (24 logs total). Stitch a cornerstone to each of these shorter logs. Randomly scatter the buttercup logs throughout the 1l and 1p log stacks. Stitch the blocks together as usual, creating randomly placed buttercups.

Block 1s
Make 1

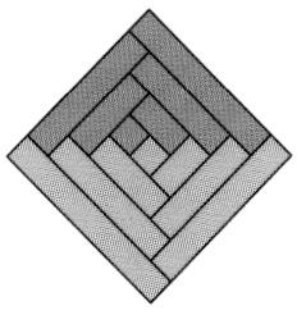

Block 1t
Make 1

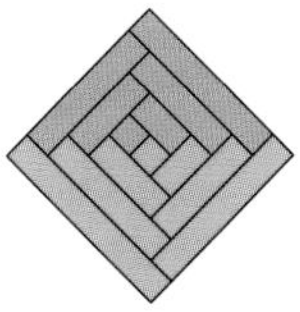

Block 1u
Make 2

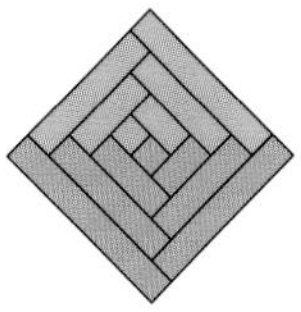

Block 1v
Make 1

Block 1w
Make 4

Block 1x
Make 1

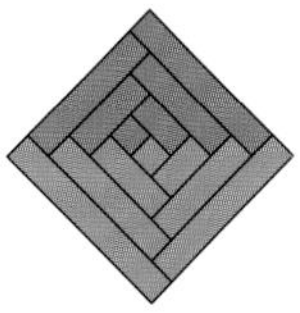

Block 1y
Make 2

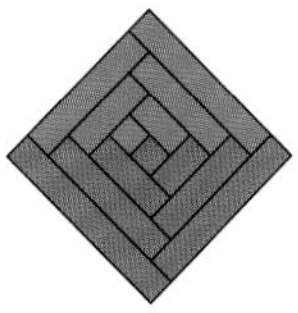

Block 1z
Make 1

Block 1aa
Make 1

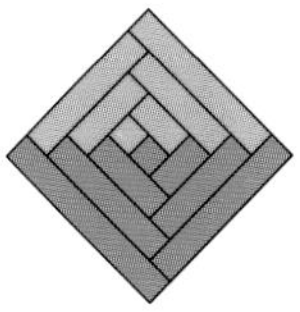

Block 1bb
Make 1

Block 1cc
Make 2

UP AT SUNRISE BLOCK 2 LOG CUTTING GUIDE

Log	Cut	Width	Length
A	7	1¼"	1¼"
B	1	1¼"	1¼"
C	1	1¼"	1¼"
D	1	1¼"	2"
E	1	1¼"	2"
F	1	1¼"	2¾"
G	1	1¼"	2¾"
H	1	1¼"	3½"
I	1	1¼"	3½"
J	1	1¼"	4¼"
K	1	1¼"	4¼"
L	1	1¼"	5"
M	1	1¼"	5"

Finished Block Size: 5¼" x 5¼"

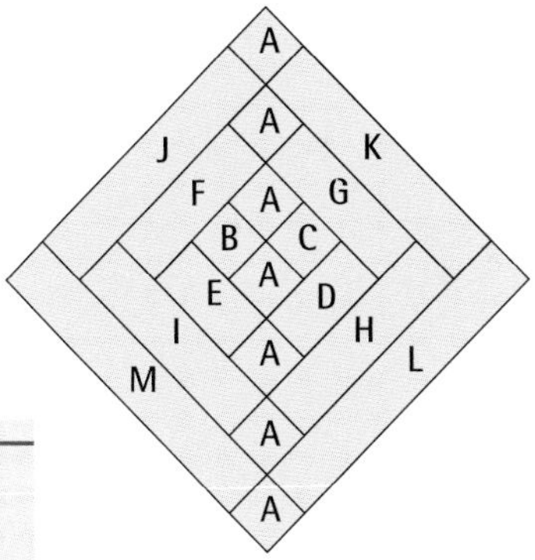

Block 2

Block 2
Make 3

Fabric Key

- light blues (sky)
- yellows (balloon)
- oranges (balloon)
- purples (balloon)
- reds (balloon)
- royal blues (balloon)
- light print (gondola)
- black/darks (rope)
- muted greens (artichokes)
- spring greens (asparagus)
- light browns/tans (ground)
- golds (wheat stubble)
- medium greens (meadow)
- yellow floral (buttercups)
- dark greens (olive trees)
- dark browns (tree trunks)
- aqua blues (sea)

UP AT SUNRISE BLOCK 3 LOG CUTTING GUIDE			
Log	Cut	Width	Length
A	4	1¼"	1¼"
B	1	1¼"	1¼"
C	1	1¼"	1¼"
D	1	1¼"	2"
E	1	1¼"	2¾"
F	1	1¼"	2¾"
G	1	1¼"	2¾"
H	1	1¼"	3½"
I	1	1¼"	4¼"
J	1	1¼"	4¼"
K	1	1¼"	4¼"
L	1	1¼"	5"
M	1	1¼"	5¾"

Finished Block Size: 5¼" x 5¼"

UP AT SUNRISE BLOCK 4 LOG CUTTING GUIDE			
Log	Cut	Width	Length
A	1	1¾"	1¾"
B	1	1¼"	1¾"
C	1	1¼"	2½"
D	1	1¼"	2½"
E	1	1¼"	3¼"
F	1	1¼"	3¼"
G	1	1¼"	4"
H	1	1¼"	4"
I	1	1¼"	4¾"
J	1	1¼"	4¾"
K	1	1¼"	5½"
L	1	1¼"	5½"
M	1	1¼"	6¼"

Finished Block Size: 5¾" x 5¾"

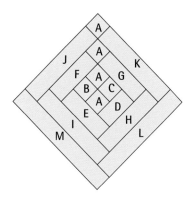

Block 3

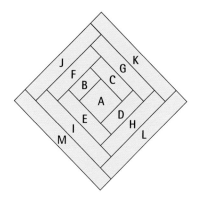

Block 4

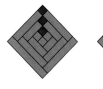

Block 3a
Make 2

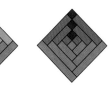

Block 3b
Make 2

Block 3c
Make 2

Block 4a
Make 6

Block 4b
Make 2

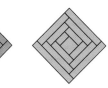

Block 4c
Make 1

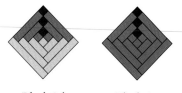

Block 3d
Make 1

Block 3e
Make 2

Block 4d
Make 2

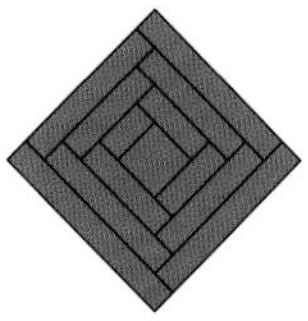

Block 4e
Make 2

Block 4f
Make 2

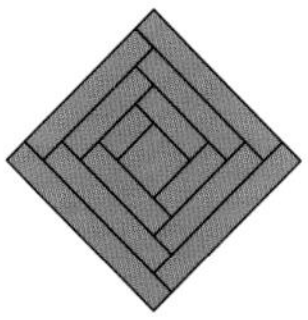

Block 4g
Make 1

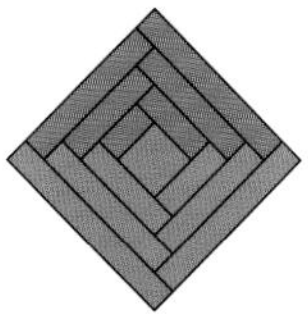

Block 4h
Make 1

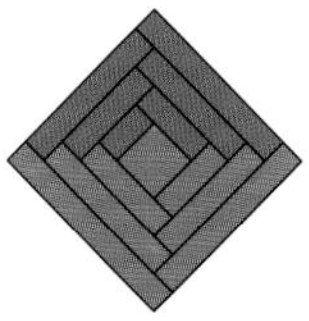

Block 4i
Make 1

Block 4j
Make 1

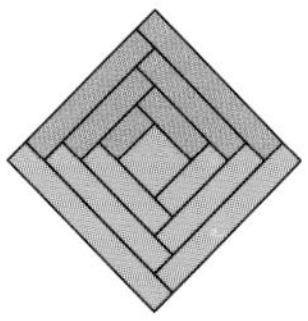

Block 4k
Make 1

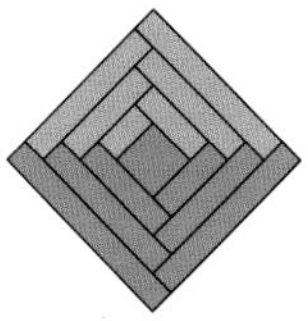

Block 4l
Make 1

Log	Cut	Width	Length
A+	1	1¾"	1¾"
A	6	1¼"	1¼"
B	1	1¼"	1¾"
C	1	1¼"	1¾"
D	1	1¼"	2½"
E	1	1¼"	2½"
F	1	1¼"	3¼"
G	1	1¼"	3¼"
H	1	1¼"	4"
I	1	1¼"	4"
J	1	1¼"	4¾"
K	1	1¼"	4¾"
L	1	1¼"	5½"
M	1	1¼"	5½"

Finished Block Size: 5¾" x 5¾"

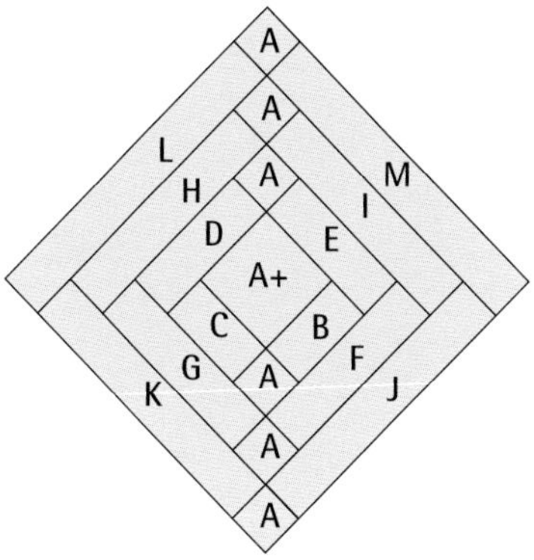

Fabric Key

- light blues (sky)
- yellows (balloon)
- oranges (balloon)
- purples (balloon)
- reds (balloon)
- royal blues (balloon)
- light print (gondola)
- black/darks (rope)
- muted greens (artichokes)
- spring greens (asparagus)
- light browns (ground)
- golds (wheat stubble)
- medium greens (meadow)
- yellow floral (buttercups)
- dark greens (olive trees)
- dark browns (tree trunks)
- aqua blues (sea)

Block 5

Block 5
Make 2

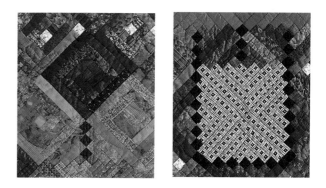

Cornerstones depict tree trunks and the gondola rope.

UP AT SUNRISE BLOCK 6 LOG CUTTING GUIDE			
Log	Cut	Width	Length
A	1	1"	1"
B	1	1"	1"
C	1	1"	1½"
D	1	1"	1½"
E	1	1"	2"
F	1	1½"	2"
G	1	1½"	3"
H	1	1"	3"
I	1	1"	3½"
J	1	1½"	3½"
K	1	1½"	4½"

Finished Block Size: 4" x 4"

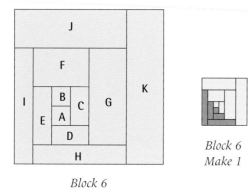

Block 6

Block 6
Make 1

ASSEMBLING THE QUILT

For general instructions, see Joining the Blocks (page 41), Making Borders (page 41), and Quilting and Finishing (page 44).

1. Lay out 136 blocks on point—124 Block 1, 3 Block 2, and 9 Block 3—as shown in the quilt diagram (page 64). Watch block orientation—some blocks are rotated when laid out. View your layout through a reducing glass to locate any blocks that are upside down or out of place. Pay close attention to blocks 2 and 3 to make sure the tree trunk and gondola rope cornerstones are oriented properly.

2. Insert blocks 4 and 5 around the edge of the layout, one at a time, following the numbering on the quilt diagram. Once you've determined the correct orientation for an edge block, cut the block in half from corner to corner, making 2 triangles. Return the appropriate triangle to the layout as a setting triangle. You will use both setting triangles from some blocks; from others only 1 triangle will fit into the design. Cut 2 of the triangles in half again for the left top and left bottom corner setting triangles.

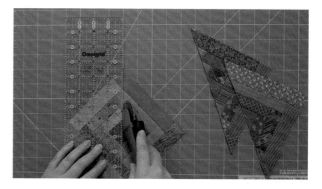

Making a setting triangle. Always double-check the orientation when cutting two-color blocks. If you cut the wrong way, the triangles won't fit the layout and they become useless.

3. Stitch the blocks and setting triangles together in diagonal rows. Press. Sew the rows together. Press.

4. Follow the Border Cutting Guide to cut the border fabrics into strips. The quilt has 3 borders and 1 corner block. Cut the inner and outer border strips lengthwise. Cut the middle border strips crosswise. Measure the quilt top to determine the final cut length of the inner borders.

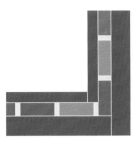

Border Corner Detail

UP AT SUNRISE BORDER CUTTING GUIDE				
Border	Fabric	Cut	Width	Length*
inner	navy	2	1¾"	63½"
		2	1¾"	69¾"
middle	balloon colors, spring green	10 assorted	2"	18"
	balloon yellow	10	1"	18"
outer	navy	2	2¾"	69"
		2	2¾"	77¼"
Block 6	navy	1	1½"	5½"
		1	1½"	4½"

*length is approximate

Sew the top and bottom inner borders to the quilt top. Press. Add the left side inner border. Press. Cut 1¼" off the end of the right side inner border. Add the border to the quilt, but instead of stitching all the way to the top, leave room for Block 6 to be inserted last.

For the middle border, cut the yellow strips into 2" segments for 90 insets (you may not use them all). Cut the spring green and balloon-colored border strips into segments that vary in length from 2½" to 4½" for 84 to 90 assorted colored bars. Stitch the colored bars and insets together alternately to make 4 long multicolor middle border strips. Measure the quilt top and adjust the colored bar piecing so that each strip is the correct length and has a yellow inset at each end. Press toward the insets. Sew the top and bottom middle borders to the quilt top. Press. Add the left side middle border. Press. Add the right side middle border, once again leaving the top right corner free for the Block 6 insertion. Press. Add the outer borders in the same sequence. Press.

Middle Border Piecing

Stitch the 4½" navy log to the top edge of Block 6. Press. Stitch the 5½" navy log to the right edge of Block 6. Press. Stitch the block to the free top edge of the borders on the right side of the quilt, aligning the right edge of the block with the right edge of the border, and stopping the stitching ¼" from the inner corner of the block. Press toward the borders. Sew the seam along the left edge of the block to complete the insertion. Press.

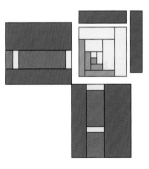

Border Corner Block

Layer and finish the quilt. Quilt the sky in curved meandering lines. In the fields use diagonal lines for furrows and short vertical lines for wheat stubble. Quilt the asparagus patch in a crosshatched pattern. Use gently undulating quilt lines on the sea. Quilt a stylized stem for each buttercup. Use outline quilting to emphasize the logs of the balloon, the trees, and the border colored bars. Use concentric lines to accentuate the sun in Block 6. Bind the edges with a 2¼"-wide bias strip cut from a 28" x 28" square of the fabric of your choice (see Binding the Quilt, page 45).

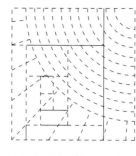

Block 6 Quilting Design

Buttercup Stem Quilting Design

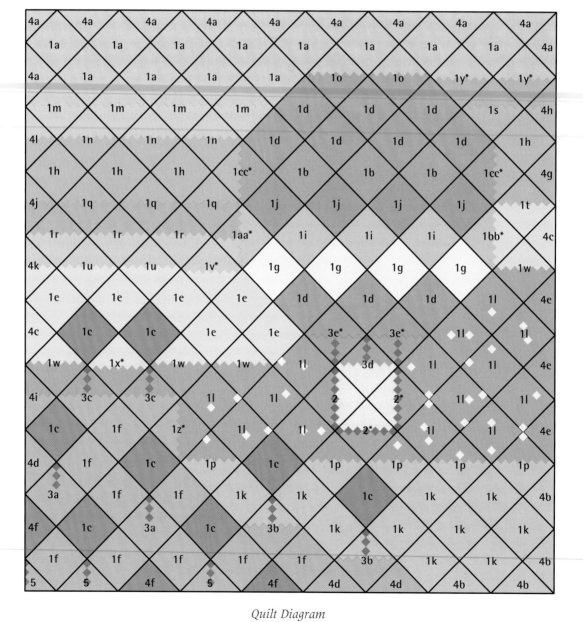

Quilt Diagram
*rotate completed block when placing

Geese in Flight

Geese in Flight, 83½" x 85½", 1981.
Machine-pieced, hand-quilted. Cottons and cotton-polyester blends, polyester batting.

Canada geese have long necks. They look well dressed in their thin white neck bands. My line drawings of geese in flight, their long necks stretched out before them, influenced my selection of a rectangular block and grid. When I turned Rectangular Courthouse Steps blocks horizontally, the scene started falling into place. It's late afternoon, the sun is soon to set, and the geese are flying low in a V formation over the marsh. Solid medium blues in varying shades play up the moody sky. Prints depict the marsh, with ugly fabrics randomly scattered where water and plants intermingle.

Canada goose in the park

Sizes *at a Glance*
QUILT: 83½" x 85½"
BLOCKS: 10" x 9"

MATERIALS

geese, border triangles		11 fat quarters assorted small-scale brown prints
geese		11 fat quarters assorted small-scale beige prints
goose necks		⅛ yard black
goose neck bands		⅛ yard white
sun		⅓ yard total assorted solid oranges
sky, border triangles		5 yards total assorted solid blues
mountains		⅝ yard total assorted grays
marsh		1¼ yards total varied-scale green prints
		⅔ yard total varied-scale blue prints
multistrip borders		2½ yards dark
		2½ yards light
backing		7½ yards (if your fabric is 45" wide, use 5 yards)
batting		87" x 89"
bias binding		1 yard dark

MAKING THE BLOCKS

For general instructions, see Rectangular Courthouse Steps Block (page 27) and Making Blocks (page 38). All log strips are cut 1½" wide. Block 1 makes up most of the quilt. Blocks 2–5 introduce slight modifications in the piecing routes. Make 56 blocks total. The geese are inserted after the blocks are constructed.

GEESE IN FLIGHT BLOCK 1 LOG CUTTING GUIDE			
Log	Cut	Width	Length
A	1	1½"	2½"
B	2	1½"	1½"
C	2	1½"	4½"
D	2	1½"	3½"
E	2	1½"	6½"
F	2	1½"	5½"
G	2	1½"	8½"
H	2	1½"	7½"
I	2	1½"	10½"

Finished Block Size: 10" x 9"

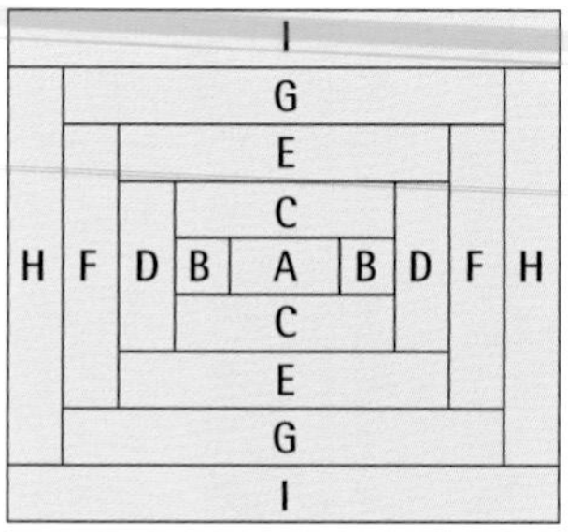

Block 1

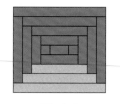

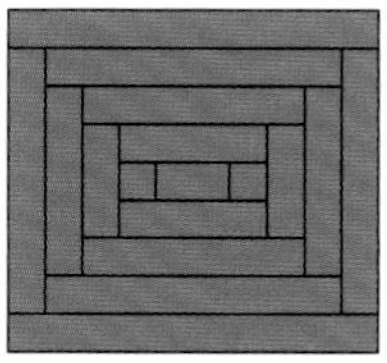

Block 1a
Make 29 all-sky blocks,
1 all-sun block,
4 all-grass blocks,
1 all-mountain block

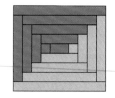

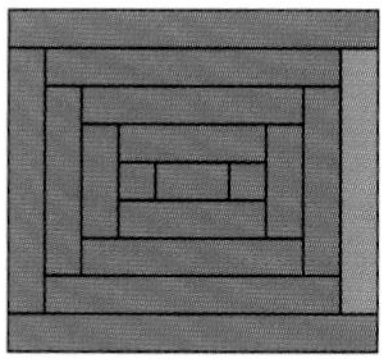

Block 1b
Make 2
Rotate 1 block 180°
when placing

Block 1c
Make 2

Block 1d
Make 1

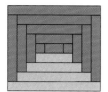

Block 1e
Make 1

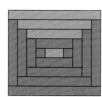

Block 1f
Make 2

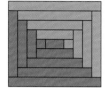

Block 1g
Make 1

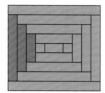

Block 1h
Make 1

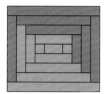

Block 1i
Make 1

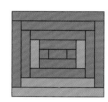

Block 1j
Make 1

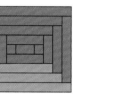

Block 1k
Make 1

Block 1l
Make 1

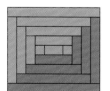

Block 1m
Make 1

Block 1n
Make 1

GEESE IN FLIGHT BLOCK 2 LOG CUTTING GUIDE

Log	Cut	Width	Length
A	3	1½"	2½"
B	2	1½"	3½"
C	2	1½"	4½"
D	2	1½"	5½"
E	2	1½"	6½"
F	2	1½"	7½"
G	2	1½"	8½"
H	2	1½"	9½"

Finished Block Size: 10" x 9"

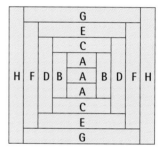

Sky/Sun Block 2

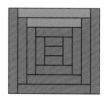

Block 2
Make 2
Rotate 1 Block 180°
when placing

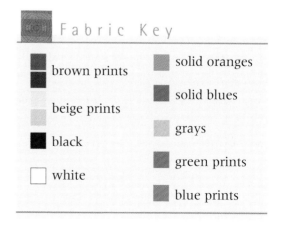

Fabric Key

brown prints

beige prints

black

white

solid oranges

solid blues

grays

green prints

blue prints

GEESE IN FLIGHT SKY/MOUNTAIN BLOCK 3 LOG CUTTING GUIDE			
Log	Cut	Width	Length
A	2	1½"	2½"
B	2	1½"	4½"
C	2	1½"	3½"
D	2	1½"	6½"
E	2	1½"	5½"
F	2	1½"	8½"
G	2	1½"	7½"
H	2	1½"	10½"

Finished Block Size: 10" x 9"

GEESE IN FLIGHT SKY/MOUNTAIN BLOCK 4 LOG CUTTING GUIDE			
Log	Cut	Width	Length
A	1	1½"	1½"
B	1	1½"	3½"
C	2	1½"	4½"
D	2	1½"	3½"
E	2	1½"	6½"
F	2	1½"	5½"
G	2	1½"	8½"
H	2	1½"	7½"
I	2	1½"	10½"

Finished Block Size: 10" x 9"

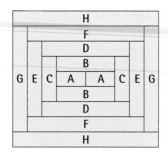

Sky/Mountain Block 3

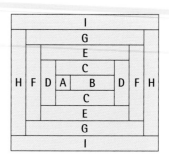

Sky/Mountain Block 4

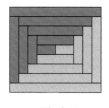

Block 3
Make 1

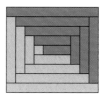

Block 4
Make 1

Fabric Key

- brown prints
- beige prints
- black
- white
- solid oranges
- solid blues
- grays
- green prints
- blue prints

GEESE IN FLIGHT SKY/MOUNTAIN BLOCK 5 LOG CUTTING GUIDE			
Log	Cut	Width	Length
A	1	1½"	2½"
B	3	1½"	1½"
C-	1	1½"	3½"
C	1	1½"	4½"
D	2	1½"	3½"
E	2	1½"	6½"
F	2	1½"	5½"
G	2	1½"	8½"
H	2	1½"	7½"
I	2	1½"	10½"

Finished Block Size: 10" x 9"

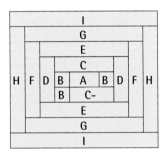

Sky/Mountain Block 5

Block 5
Make 1

INSERTING THE GEESE

1. Make geese templates A through I (page 73). Use templates A through G to cut 63 pieces.

Template	Cut	Fabric
A	9	black
B	9	white
C	9	black
D	9	white
E	9	assorted browns
F	9	8 assorted blues, 1 gray
G	9	assorted beiges

2. Cut 11 assorted brown 1" x 16" strips. Stitch the strips together, side by side. Press. Use templates H and I to mark 5 H front wings and 4 I back wings on the strip set. Staystitch ⅛" in from the marked outlines to stabilize each shape. Carefully cut out each wing on the outline.

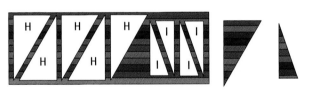

Wing Cutting Diagram
Brown Strip Set

Wing H
Make 5

Wing I
Make 4

3. Cut 11 assorted beige 1" x 14" strips. Repeat Step 2 to make a beige strip set. Use templates H and I *in reverse* to mark 4 mirror-image H wings and 5 mirror-image I wings. Staystitch the wings and cut them out.

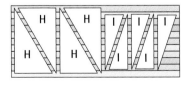

Wing Cutting Diagram
Beige Strip Set

Wing H
(in reverse)
Make 4

Wing I
(in reverse)
Make 5

4. Lay out goose body pieces A through F in a horizontal line, as shown. Stitch together. Press toward the darker fabric. Make 9 units total.

Goose Body
Make 9

5. Select 9 Block 1a's (8 all-sky and 1 all-mountain) for dissection. Lay a block flat, face side up. Place a goose body, face side up, at the top, bottom, or middle of the block. (One exception: On the all-mountain block, position the goose in the middle, so that the wings will fall above the marsh.) Mark a small dot on each side edge of the block, even with the middle of the goose body strip. Set the goose body aside. Draw a horizontal line across the block, connecting the dots. Draw parallel lines ¼" above and below the first drawn line. Cut on the two outer lines, removing a ½"-wide strip. Discard the strip, leaving behind the upper and lower sections of the block. Dissect 9 blocks total.

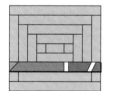

1. *Position the Goose Body*   **2.** *Mark 2 Dots*

3. *Draw 3 Lines*   **4.** *Complete the Dissection*

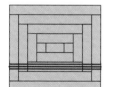

stitching lines for inset

Examples of Dissected Blocks

6. Align a goose body on the dissected edge of an upper block section, face sides together. Stitch, using a ¼" seam. Press the seam allowance toward the goose body. Align Piece G (the goose belly) face side up on the dissected edge of the lower block section. Appliqué the curved edge, leaving the top raw edge free.

7. Press under the two longer edges of a brown Wing H, to prepare the piece for appliqué. Position the wing facedown on the goose body (the upper block section), raw edges aligned. Position the lower block section on top, face sides together, sandwiching the wing in between. Stitch. Press toward the goose body.

8. Flatten the brown wing onto the lower block section. Position a beige Wing I underneath Wing H. Turn under the visible raw edges of Wing I and appliqué in place. Appliqué the pressed edges of Wing H. If the wings extend beyond the block edge, wait until the blocks are joined in rows to complete the appliqué. Repeat steps 7 and 8 to make 5 "wings-down" blocks. For a realistic look, vary the wing placement slightly from goose to goose.

Goose with wings down, and goose with wings up

9. Repeat Step 7 to prepare each beige Wing H for the "wings-up" goose blocks. Position a wing facedown on the goose belly (the lower block section), raw edges aligned. Position the upper block section on top, face sides together, sandwiching the wing in between. Stitch. Press toward the goose belly. Press Wing H up, and slip

a brown Wing I underneath. Appliqué both wings in place, as in Step 8.

ASSEMBLING THE QUILT

For general instructions, see Joining the Blocks (page 41), Making Borders (page 41), and Quilting and Finishing (page 44).

1. Lay out 56 blocks in 8 rows of 7 blocks each, as shown in the quilt photograph (page 65) and quilt diagram (page 72).

2. Stitch the blocks in horizontal rows. Press. Join the rows, taking care not to catch any loose wings in the seams. Press. Flatten all loose wings onto the blocks and appliqué.

3. Follow the Border Cutting Guide (page 72) to cut the Flying Geese border strips *only*. (The remaining strips will be cut later.) Cut the brown strips into 69 squares 3½" x 3½". Cut the squares diagonally in half in both directions to create 276 quarter-square triangles (A). Cut the sky blue strips into 276 squares 2" x 2". Cut the squares diagonally in half to create 552 half-square triangles (B).

4. Randomly sort and stack Flying Geese A and B triangles to obtain a mix. Join B triangles to each short side of an A triangle to construct one Flying Geese unit, as shown. Make 276 units. Press seams toward the B triangle.

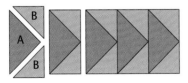

Flying Geese Units
Make 276

5. Stitch the Flying Geese units together, with all the geese "flying" in the same direction, to make 2 strips with 33 units, 2 strips with 35 units, and 2 strips with 70 units. Press all seams toward the base of triangle A. Join the two 33-unit strips so the geese fly out from the center (the bottom Flying Geese border). Join the two 35-unit strips so the geese fly in toward the center (the top Flying Geese border). Press.

6. Measure the quilt top and the Flying Geese borders. Double-check the measurements against the Border Cutting Guide. Recalculate the width and length of the light and dark inner border strips, so that the Flying Geese borders will come together exactly. Cut the inner and outer border strips, as listed in the guide, using your recalculations.

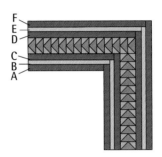

Border Corner Detail

7. Sew the dark A shorter inner border strips to the top and bottom edges of the quilt top. Press. Sew the dark A longer inner border strips to the side edges. (For ease of construction, the

Border	Fabric	Cut	Width	Length*
Inner A	dark	2	1⅜"*	70½"
		2	1⅜"*	74¼"
Inner B	light	2	⅞"*	72¼"
		2	⅞"*	75"
Inner C	dark	2	1⅜"*	73"
		2	1⅜"*	76¾"
Flying	browns	14	3½"	18"
Geese	blues	31	2"	18"
Outer D	dark	2	1⅜"	79¼"
		2	1⅜"	83"
Outer E	light	2	⅞"	81"
		2	⅞"	83¾"
Outer F	dark	2	1⅜"	81¾"
		2	1⅜"	85½"

*measurement is approximate

corners are butted instead of mitered.) Add the light B and dark C inner borders in the same sequence, pressing after each addition. Stitch the bottom Flying Geese border to the quilt top. Press. Add the side Flying Geese borders so that the geese fly up both sides of the quilt top, as shown in the quilt photograph (page 65). Press. Add the top Flying Geese border. Press. Add the dark D outer top and bottom borders first. Press. Add the dark D sides and press. Add the light E and dark F outer borders in the same order.

8. Layer and finish the quilt. Quilt horizontal lines across the sky, as the geese fly, to represent smooth and peaceful flight patterns. Outline-quilt the geese, marsh, and borders near the ditch, to emphasize each log. Quilt the sun with concentric circles, and use dense vertical quilting on the mountains. Bind the edges of the quilt with a 2¼"-wide bias strip cut from a 30" x 30" square of the fabric of your choice (see Binding the Quilt, page 45).

1a**	1a	1a	1a	1a	2	1a
1a	1a**	1a	1a	1b	1a	1b
1a	1a	1a**	1a*	1a	2	1a
1a	1a	1a	1a	1a*	1a**	1a
1a	1c	1a*	1a**	1a	1a	1a
3	1a*	4	1c	1d	5	1e
1a	1i	1j	1k	1l	1a	1a
1f	1h	1g	1n	1m	1f	1a

Quilt Diagram
*insert goose, wings up **insert goose, wings down

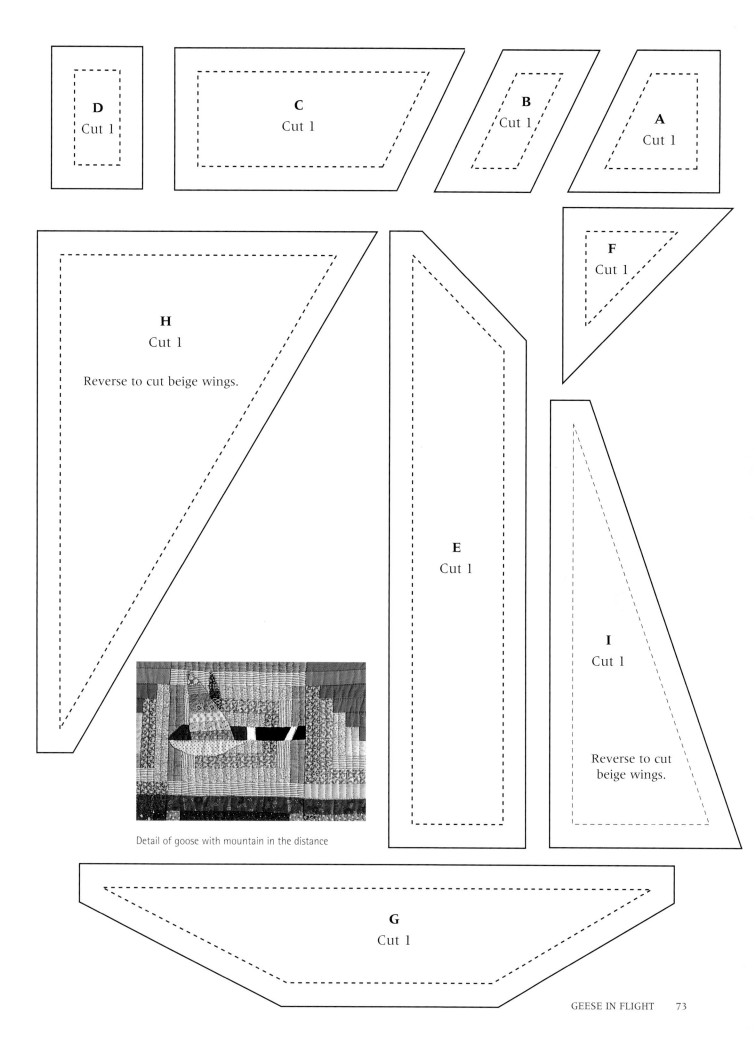

D
Cut 1

C
Cut 1

B
Cut 1

A
Cut 1

F
Cut 1

H
Cut 1

Reverse to cut beige wings.

E
Cut 1

I
Cut 1

Reverse to cut beige wings.

Detail of goose with mountain in the distance

G
Cut 1

Hilltop Houses

Hilltop Houses, 37½" x 37½", 1987.
Machine-pieced, hand-quilted. Cottons, polyester batting.

This wall quilt was inspired by a photograph of homes in Daly City, California. The hillside setting is recognizable to anyone driving into San Francisco from the airport, south of the city. I designed *Hilltop Houses* for a quilt challenge at Silver Dollar City in Branson, Missouri. We were directed to choose our fabrics from a collection from Springs Industries—I used every fabric available to get as much variety as possible! The challenge guidelines also determined the small size of the quilt. Each block is 2½" x 2½" square, with ½" finished logs. Redrafting the block with ¾" logs increases its size to 3¾" x 3¾" square, and the quilt becomes 55" x 55".

Sizes
at a Glance
QUILT: 37½" x 37½"
BLOCKS: 2½" x 2½"

Homes along the expressway, Daly City, California

MATERIALS

houses, roofs, windows — 2 fat quarters beige/brown prints or solids

4 fat quarters pink/rose prints or solids

4 fat quarters navy blue prints or solids

3 fat quarters light blue prints or solids

3 fat quarters dark green prints or solids

3 fat quarters light green prints or solids

chimneys — 1 fat quarter dark solid

sky — ¼ yard solid blue

borders, bias binding — 1⅛ yards dark print

batting — 41" x 41"

backing — 1¼ yards

Fabric note: A fat quarter is ¼ yard of fabric, but it measures 18" x 22" instead of 9" x 44". Instead of a long, narrow rectangle, you're working with a shape that's almost square. In this project, use each fat quarter for several houses, with the leftover fabric going for the roofs, windows, and doors of neighboring houses. Look for patterns and stripes that will vary in appearance when cut on the lengthwise and crosswise grains. Add more fat quarters or scraps for even greater variety.

MAKING THE BLOCKS

For general instructions, see Traditional Log Cabin Block (page 22), and Making Blocks (page 38). Refer to the quilt diagram (page 77) to select fabrics for each house, roof, and window. Strive for contrast between a house and its windows, and also between neighboring houses. Once you've chosen your colors, cut the logs

block by block, following the block diagrams and log cutting guides. Note that the cut log lengths are the same throughout. The three block variations are due to differences in the piecing order. Block 2 is pieced counterclockwise, and Block 3 has an internal piecing variation to accommodate the chimney. Make 196 blocks total.

HILLTOP HOUSES BLOCK 1 LOG CUTTING GUIDE			
Log	Cut	Width	Length
A	1	1"	1"
B	1	1"	1"
C	1	1"	1½"
D	1	1"	1½"
E	1	1"	2"
F	1	1"	2"
G	1	1"	2½"
H	1	1"	2½"
I	1	1"	3"

Finished Block Size: 2½" x 2½"

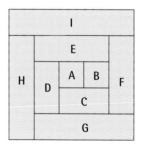

Block 1

Block 1a
Window
Make 111 assorted

Block 1b
Sky
Make 7

Block 1c
Left Door
Make 1

HILLTOP HOUSES BLOCK 2 LOG CUTTING GUIDE			
Log	Cut	Width	Length
A	1	1"	1"
B	1	1"	1"
C	1	1"	1½"
D	1	1"	1½"
E	1	1"	2"
F	1	1"	2"
G	1	1"	2½"
H	1	1"	2½"
I	1	1"	3"

Finished Block Size: 2½" x 2½"

HILLTOP HOUSES BLOCK 3 LOG CUTTING GUIDE			
Log	Cut	Width	Length
A	1	1"	1"
B	1	1"	1"
C	1	1"	1½"
D	1	1"	1½"
E	1	1"	2"
F	1	1"	2"
G	1	1"	2½"
H	1	1"	2½"
I	1	1"	3"

Finished Block Size: 2½" x 2½"

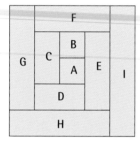

Block 2

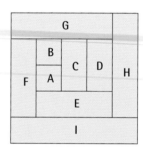

Block 3

Block 2a
Left Roof
Make 37 assorted

Block 2b
Right Door
Make 3 assorted

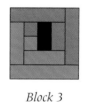

Block 3
Right Roof/Chimney
Make 37 assorted

Detail of Houses and Roofs

Fabric Key

☐ beiges/browns	■ dark greens
■ pinks/roses	☐ light greens
■ navy blues	■ dark solid
■ light blues	■ solid blue

ASSEMBLING THE QUILT

For general instructions, see Joining the Blocks (page 41), Making Borders (page 41), and Quilting and Finishing (page 44).

1. Lay out 196 blocks in 14 rows of 14 blocks each, as shown in the quilt photograph (page 74) and quilt diagram (page 77). Double-check the block placement house by house, and adjust as needed.

2. Stitch the blocks together in rows. Press. Join the rows. Press.

3. Measure the quilt top to determine the lengths of the border strips. From the dark print fabric, cut 2 lengthwise 1½" x 35½" strips (or the appropriate length) for the top and bottom borders, and 2 lengthwise 1½" x 37½" strips (or the appropriate length) for the side borders. Sew the top and bottom border strips to the quilt top. Press. Sew the side borders to the quilt top. Press.

4. Layer and finish the quilt. One quilting option is to stitch near the ditch along the seam lines of the blocks and the center squares. Quilt free-flowing lines for clouds in the sky area, without regard to the logs. Bind the edges with a 2⅛"-wide bias strip cut from a 20" x 20" square of the same fabric you used for the border (see Binding the Quilt, page 45).

Quilt Diagram

Row Houses

San Francisco's Painted Ladies

Row Houses, 82½" x 106½", 1985.
Machine-pieced, hand-quilted. Cottons, polyester batting.
Selected as one of the twentieth century's 100 best American quilts.
Shown at the 1999 International Quilt Festival in Houston, Texas.

Sizes
at a Glance
QUILT: 82½" x 106½"

**LOG CABIN
 BLOCKS:** 4½" x 4½"

**PAINT CHIP
 BLOCKS:** 3" x 3"

A 1979 trip to San Francisco for the Patch in Time #4 quilt conference also introduced me to the Painted Ladies. This lovely group of Victorian row houses sits across from Alamo Square, between Golden Gate Park and downtown San Francisco. Known worldwide for their sophisticated style, colors, and intricate detail, the houses are even more intriguing when you actually see them. Without my camera to document the sight, I purchased a postcard for future design reference. I envisioned myself depicting these lovely houses in appliqué and embroidery—someday.

Years went by. One afternoon, while I was sketching on the edge of a legal pad, a repetitive line drawing of the Painted Ladies began to appear in rows.

No Victorian ornamentation or curved scroll work here; just a simple structure that could be patched in Log Cabin. My desire to begin sewing clashed head-on with reality. There could be no quilting for me until we completed our "real" house building. Still, one can hope and dream. With each trip to the paint store, I looked at—drooled over, actually—a "historical colors" paint brochure. Noting my perpetual interest in the brochure's bright, boldly colored paint chips, the store owner one day asked me if I would like to have it! I left the store that day with gallons of pale ivory paint and a priceless, colorful design source. Five years after first seeing the Painted Ladies, the sketch of row houses practically leaped from my design folder. I had no dilemma about a color plan. The paint chips were an instant answer.

The moral of this story: Even when the immediate situation won't allow you to quilt, be alert to design possibilities. Lock in ideas by sketching, photographing, or simply noting inspirations. Tell yourself, "I must keep this idea," and then follow through. Don't rely on memory alone. Tangible reminders, even if buried deep in a folder, can inspire future designs. Let your mind's creative meanderings connect the dots between disparate design ideas. Drawings on a napkin, doodling on the edge of a legal pad, notes in a journal, or paint chips in a folder are potential sparks, ready to ignite into a composition.

MATERIALS

sky		1 yard total assorted blues
houses, paint chips		4 yards total assorted brights, including green, red, yellow, blue, dusty pinks, orange, and brown
roofs, chimneys, paint chip logs		2⅝ yards total assorted darks and medium grays
windows		⅜ yard assorted lights and darks
doors, transoms window boxes		⅝ yard assorted brights and darks
sashing, inner/ outer border		3⅛ yards dark stripe
inner/outer multistrip borders		3 yards black stripe
inner multistrip border		2⅝ yards dusty pink
outer multistrip border		3 yards gray print
backing		7¼ yards (if your fabric is 45" wide, use 6¼ yards)
batting		86" x 110"
bias binding		1 yard dark

Fabric note: Choose fabric colors that will provide maximum contrast between the houses, windows, doors, and roofs.

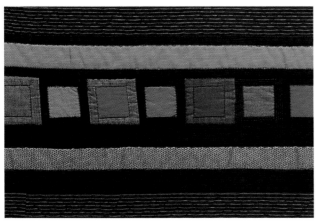

A multicolor border includes Paint Chip blocks.

MAKING THE BLOCKS

For general instructions, see Traditional Log Cabin Block (page 22), Offset Center Variation Block (page 24), and Making Blocks (page 38). Refer to the quilt diagram (page 87) to select fabrics for each house, roof, and window. Once you've chosen your colors, cut the logs block by block, following the block diagrams and log cutting guides. Sew the blocks in pairs to form units, building each house one story at a time. Most blocks have a standard clockwise piecing route, but some blocks change direction one or more times to accommodate a door or chimney. Make 192 blocks total, or enough for 22 whole houses and 4 half-houses. Use the leftover fabrics to make 104 Paint Chip blocks.

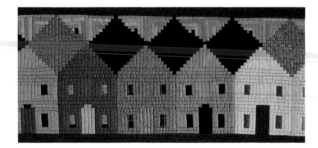

Seven different first floor units create variety in the doors and windows. The upper story and roof units are the same for every house, except for the colors.

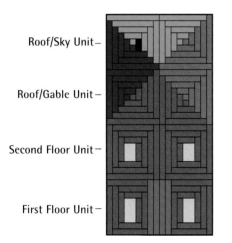

Roof/Sky Unit —
Roof/Gable Unit —
Second Floor Unit —
First Floor Unit —

Block Placement Diagram

Even though this 8-block layout is a full repeat, it doesn't depict a complete house. A neighboring house is needed to the left to complete the slanting roof, which falls to the left of the gable. At times, the roofs may appear to fall to the right of the gable. This illusionary quality is fascinating when the quilt is on a bed.

ROW HOUSES ROOF/SKY UNIT LOG CUTTING GUIDE				
Fabric	Log	Cut	Width	Length
roof	A	2	1"	1"
	D	2	1"	1½"
	E	1	1"	2"
	G	1	1"	2½"
	H	2	1"	2½"
	I	1	1"	3"
	K	1	1"	3½"
	L	2	1"	3½"
	M	1	1"	4"
	O	1	1"	4½"
	P	2	1"	4½"
	Q	1	1"	5"
chimney	C	1	1"	1 ½"
sky	B	2	1"	1"
	C	1	1"	1½"
	E	1	1"	2"
	F	2	1"	2"
	G	1	1"	2½"
	I	1	1"	3"
	J	2	1"	3"
	K	1	1"	3½"
	M	1	1"	4"
	N	2	1"	4"
	O	1	1"	4½"
	Q	1	1"	5"

Finished Block Size: 4½" x 4½"

Fabric Key

blues	dark stripe
brights	black stripe
darks/mediums	dusty pink
lights	grays

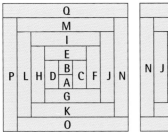

Roof/Sky Unit

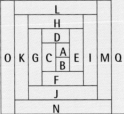

Roof/Sky Unit
Make 22 assorted units
and 4 half units (2 of each)

Roofing Tip

To streamline the roof assembly, cut all the roof logs for one roof/sky unit or one roof/gable unit from the same roof fabric. Sort the logs by letter according to the block diagrams. Label the roof logs from the two right-hand blocks, and set them aside to use later, in the house to the left. Keep the exchange going until you have assembled enough roof logs for all the houses.

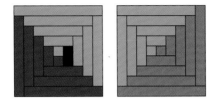

Roof/Gable Unit

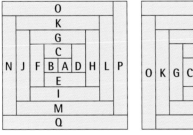

Roof/Gable Unit
Make 22 assorted units
and 4 half units (2 of each)

Fabric	Log	Cut	Width	Length
house	A	1	1"	1"
	B	1	1"	1"
	C	1	1"	1½"
	D	1	1"	1½"
	E	1	1"	2"
	F	1	1"	2"
	G	1	1"	2½"
	H	1	1"	2½"
	I	1	1"	3"
	J	1	1"	3"
	K	1	1"	3½"
	L	1	1"	3½"
	M	1	1"	4"
	N	1	1"	4"
	O	1	1"	4½"
	P	1	1"	4½"
	Q	1	1"	5"
roof	A	1	1"	1"
	B	1	1"	1"
	C	1	1"	1½"
	D	1	1"	1½"
	E	1	1"	2"
	F	1	1"	2"
	G	1	1"	2½"
	H	1	1"	2½"
	I	1	1"	3"
	J	1	1"	3"
	K	1	1"	3½"
	L	1	1"	3½"
	M	1	1"	4"
	N	1	1"	4"
	O	1	1"	4½"
	P	1	1"	4½"
	Q	1	1"	5"

Finished Block Size: 4½" x 4½"

Row Houses Second Floor Unit Log Cutting Guide				
Fabric	Log	Cut	Width	Length
window	A	2	1½"	2"
house	B	2	1"	2"
	C	2	1"	2"
	D	2	1"	2½"
	E	2	1"	2½"
	F	2	1"	3"
	G	2	1"	3"
	H	2	1"	3½"
	I	2	1"	3½"
	J	2	1"	4"
	K	2	1"	4"
	L	2	1"	4½"
	M	2	1"	4½"
	N	2	1"	5"

Finished Block Size: 4½" x 4½"

Row Houses First Floor Unit 1 Log Cutting Guide				
Fabric	Log	Cut	Width	Length
window	A	2	1½"	2½"
house	B	2	1"	2½"
	E	2	1"	2½"
	C	2	1"	2"
	D	2	1"	3"
	G	2	1"	3"
	F	2	1"	3½"
	I	2	1"	3½"
	H	2	1"	4"
	K	2	1"	4"
	J	2	1"	4½"
door	L	2	1"	5"
	M	2	1"	5"

Finished Block Size: 4½" x 4½"

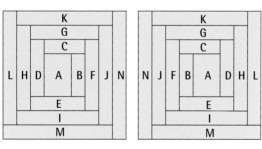

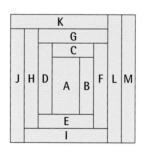

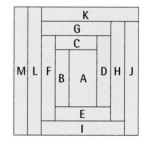

Second Floor Unit

First Floor Unit 1

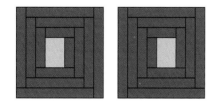

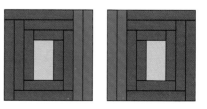

Second Floor Unit
Make 22 assorted units
and 4 half units (2 of each)

First Floor Unit 1
Make 5 assorted units and 2 half units
(for left and right sides of Row 1)

ROW HOUSES FIRST FLOOR UNIT 2 LOG CUTTING GUIDE				
Fabric	Log	Cut	Width	Length
window	A	2	1½"	2 ½"
house	B	2	1"	2½"
	C	2	1"	2"
	D	2	1"	3"
	E	2	1"	2½"
	F	2	1"	3½"
	G	2	1"	3"
	H	2	1"	4"
	I	2	1"	3½"
	K	2	1"	4½"
	L	2	1"	4½"
door	J	2	1"	4½"
	M	2	1"	5"

Finished Block Size: 4½" x 4½"

ROW HOUSES FIRST FLOOR UNIT 3 LOG CUTTING GUIDE				
Fabric	Log	Cut	Width	Length
window	A	2	1½"	2½"
house	B	2	1"	2½"
	E	2	1"	2½"
	C	2	1"	2"
	D	2	1"	3"
	G	2	1"	3"
	F	2	1"	3½"
	I	2	1"	3½"
	H	2	1"	4"
	J	2	1"	4½"
	K	2	1"	4½"
door	L	2	1"	4½"
	M	2	1"	4½"
transom	N	2	1"	1"

Finished Block Size: 4½" x 4½"

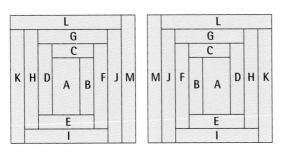

First Floor Unit 2

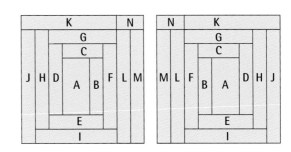

First Floor Unit 3

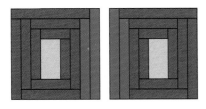

First Floor Unit 2
Make 6 assorted

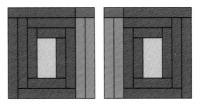

First Floor Unit 3
Make 1

Fabric	Log	Cut	Width	Length
window	A	2	1½"	2"
window box	B	2	1"	1½"
house	C	2	1"	2½"
	F	2	1"	2½"
	D	2	1"	2"
	E	2	1"	3"
	H	2	1"	3"
	I	2	1"	4"
	G	2	1"	3 ½"
	J	2	1"	3½"
	L	2	1"	4½"
	M	2	1"	4½"
door	K	2	1"	4½"
	N	2	1"	5"

Finished Block Size: 4½" x 4½"

Fabric	Log	Cut	Width	Length
window	A	2	1½"	2"
window box	B	2	1"	1½"
house	C	2	1"	2½"
	F	2	1"	2½"
	D	2	1"	2"
	E	2	1"	3"
	H	2	1"	3"
	G	2	1"	3½"
	J	2	1"	3½"
	I	2	1"	4"
	L	2	1"	4"
	K	2	1"	4½"
door	M	2	1"	4½"
	N	2	1"	4½"
transom	O	2	1"	1½"

Finished Block Size: 4½" x 4½"

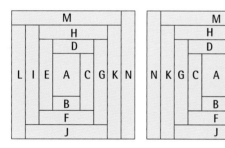

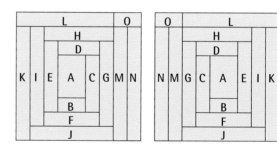

First Floor Unit 4

First Floor Unit 5

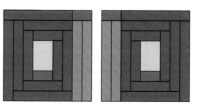

First Floor Unit 4
Make 4 assorted

First Floor Unit 5
Make 3 assorted

ROW HOUSES FIRST FLOOR UNIT 6 LOG CUTTING GUIDE				
Fabric	Log	Cut	Width	Length
window	A	2	1½"	2"
window box	B	2	1"	1 ½"
house	C	2	1"	2 ½"
	F	2	1"	2½"
	D	2	1"	2"
	E	2	1"	3"
	H	2	1"	3"
	G	2	1"	3½"
	J	2	1"	3½"
	I	2	1"	4"
	L	2	1"	4"
	K	2	1"	4½"
door	M	2	1"	5"
	N	2	1"	5"

Finished Block Size: 4½" x 4½"

ROW HOUSES FIRST FLOOR UNIT 7 LOG CUTTING GUIDE				
Fabric	Log	Cut	Width	Length
window	A	2	2"	2"
house	B	2	1"	2"
	C	2	1"	2½"
	D	2	1"	2½"
	E	2	1"	3"
	F	2	1"	3"
	G	2	1"	3½"
	H	2	1"	3½"
	I	2	1"	4"
	J	2	1"	4"
	M	2	1"	5"
door	K	2	1"	4½"
	L	2	1"	4½"

Finished Block Size: 4½" x 4½"

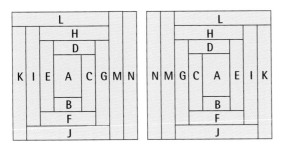

First Floor Unit 6

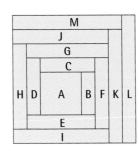

First Floor Unit 7

*First Floor Unit 6
Make 2 units and 1 half unit
(for left side of Row 3)*

*First Floor Unit 7
Make 1 unit and 1 half unit
(for right side of Row 3)*

ROW HOUSES PAINT CHIP BLOCK LOG CUTTING GUIDE

Fabric	Log	Cut	Width	Length
assorted house	A	1	2½"	2½"
assorted roof	B	1	1"	2½"
	C	1	1"	3"
	D	1	1"	3"
	E	1	1"	3½"

Finished Block Size: 3" x 3"

Paint Chip Block

*Paint Chip Block
Make 104 assorted*

ASSEMBLING THE QUILT

For general instructions, see Joining the Blocks (page 41), Making Borders (page 41), and Quilting and Finishing (page 44).

1. Lay out 176 house blocks (88 units) in 4 rows as shown in the quilt photograph (page 78) and quilt diagram (page 87). Add the 16 half-unit blocks for the half-houses at the ends of rows 1 and 3. Make sure all of the roof blocks that fall to the left of each gable are the same color fabric. Follow the quilt diagram to vary the placement of first floor units 1–7.

2. Sew the block pairs together into units. Press. Sew 4 units together in a column for each house; make 22 houses total. Press. Sew the half units together in columns to make the 4 half-houses. Press. Join the houses and half-houses together in 4 rows. Press.

3. Cut 3 lengthwise 2½" x 54½" strips from the dark stripe fabric for the horizontal sashing. Join the house rows together, inserting the sashing strips in between. Press.

4. Stitch the Paint Chip blocks together at random, varying the colors. Make 2 strips with 21 blocks each for the top and bottom middle borders, and 2 strips with 31 blocks each for the side middle borders. Press.

5. Measure the quilt top and the middle borders. Double-check the measurements in the Border Cutting Guide: Recalculate the width and length of the dark stripe inner border, if necessary, so that once you've added the multistrip inner border, the Paint Chip blocks will fit together exactly. Cut the border strips lengthwise, as listed

ROW HOUSES BORDER CUTTING GUIDE

Border	Fabric	Cut	Width	Length*
inner	dark stripe	2	2½"*	54½"
		2	2½"*	82½"
inner black multistrip	stripe	2	1"	68"
		2	1"	92"
	dusty pink	2	2"	68"
		2	2"	93"
	black stripe	2	1"	68"
		2	1"	92"
outer black multistrip	stripe	2	2"	83"
		2	2"	107"
	gray print	2	2"	83"
		2	2"	107"
	black stripe	2	2"	83"
		2	2"	107"
outer	dark stripe	2	2½"	78½"
		2	2½"	106½"

*measurement is approximate

in the guide, using your recalculations. Sew the appropriate strips together to make 4 black stripe/dusty pink/black stripe inner multistrip borders, and 4 black stripe/gray print/black stripe outer multistrip borders.

6. Sew the top and bottom inner borders to the quilt top. Press. Add the side inner borders. Press. Add the multistrip inner borders, mitering the corners. Press. Add the top and bottom middle borders (the Paint Chip blocks). Press. Add the side middle borders (the Paint Chip blocks). Press. Add the multistrip outer borders, mitering the corners. Press. Add the top and bottom outer borders. Press. Add the side outer borders. Press.

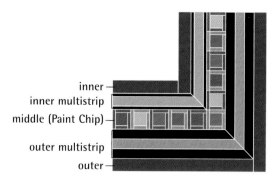

Border Corner Detail

7. Layer and finish the quilt. Quilt a diagonal square grid in the sashing and outer border. Outline-quilt along the sashing and border seams, and the Paint Chip blocks. Bind the edges with a 2¼"-wide bias strip cut from a 32" x 32" square of the same fabric you used in the outer border (see Binding the Quilt, page 45).

Numbers indicate first floor block variations.

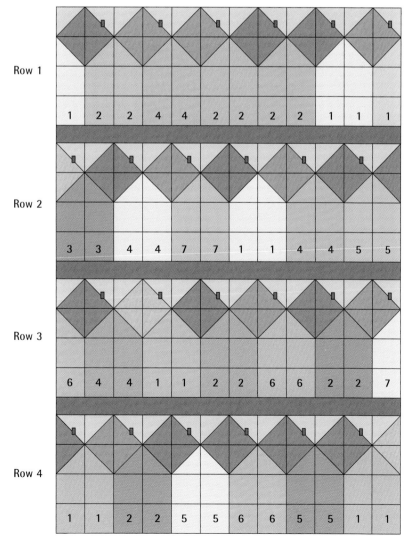

Row 1

| 1 | 2 | 2 | 4 | 4 | 2 | 2 | 2 | 2 | 1 | 1 | 1 |

Row 2

| 3 | 3 | 4 | 4 | 7 | 7 | 1 | 1 | 4 | 4 | 5 | 5 |

Row 3

| 6 | 4 | 4 | 1 | 1 | 2 | 2 | 6 | 6 | 2 | 2 | 7 |

Row 4

| 1 | 1 | 2 | 2 | 5 | 5 | 6 | 6 | 5 | 5 | 1 | 1 |

Quilt Diagram

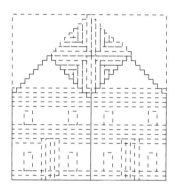

Quilting Detail

Carolina Row

Carolina Row, 66" x 47½", 2000.
Machine-pieced, hand-quilted. Cottons, polyester batting.

A walk along the waterfront in Charleston, South Carolina, rewards you with a view of lovely historic homes. These well-preserved architectural monuments are privately owned homes with present-day relevance. Aligned side by side, they express a lively sense of community. Color inspiration abounds, providing glorious options for a quilt.

To depict these tall, stylized homes, I chose rectangular blocks, which I stacked vertically. All the blocks are the same width, but the lengths vary according to the center log dimensions. Another way to play with the height and diagonal line of a block is to drop the final wide log from one block, and let it share the end log of the adjoining block. I call this technique Log Share (see page 32). Look closely where the roof/sky blocks join the house/roof blocks to see how it works.

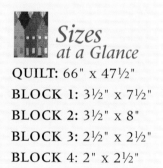

Sizes
at a Glance

QUILT: 66" x 47½"
BLOCK 1: 3½" x 7½"
BLOCK 2: 3½" x 8"
BLOCK 3: 2½" x 2½"
BLOCK 4: 2" x 2½"

Historic homes in Charleston, South Carolina

MATERIALS

houses	8 fat quarters in assorted muted hues (2 blue, 2 purple, 2 orange, and 2 green)
roofs, border logs, door steps	1⅜ yards total assorted grays
sky	1¼ yards total assorted pale blues
windows, doors, border chips	⅝ yard total assorted brights
inner border	⅓ yard yellow
outer border, backing	3 yards multicolored print
batting	69" x 51"
bias binding	¾ yard print

MAKING THE BLOCKS

For general instructions, see Traditional Log Cabin Block (page 22), Elongated Courthouse Steps Block (page 28), and Making Blocks (page 38). Refer to the quilt diagram (page 92) to select fabrics for each house, roof, and window. Strive for contrast between neighboring houses and roofs. Once you've chosen your colors, cut the logs block by block, following the block diagrams and log cutting guides. Refer to the block placement diagram to organize and label the completed blocks for each house repeat. Make 80 blocks total, enough for 8 houses. Use the leftover fabrics to make 90 blocks for the middle border.

CAROLINA ROW BLOCK 1 LOG CUTTING GUIDE			
Log	**Cut**	**Width**	**Length**
A	1	1"	2"
B	2	1"	2"
C	2	1½"	2"
D	2	1"	4"
E	2	1½"	3"
F	2	1"	6"
G	2	1½"	4"

Finished Block Size: 3½" x 7½"

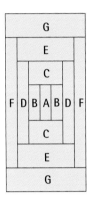

Block 1

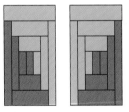

Roof/Sky
Block 1a   Block 1b
Make 8   Make 8
Discard Log G (a Log Share block)

Roof/Gable
Block 1c   Block 1d
Make 8   Make 8

Second Floor
Block 1e
Make 16

CAROLINA ROW BLOCK 2 LOG CUTTING GUIDE			
Log	Cut	Width	Length
A	1	1"	2½"
B	2	1"	2½"
C	2	1½"	2"
D	2	1"	4½"
E	2	1½"	3"
F	2	1"	6½"
G	2	1½"	4"

Finished Block Size: 3½" x 8"

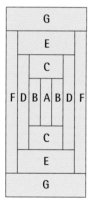

Block 2

Sky
Block 2a
Make 16

First Floor
Block 2b   *Block 2c*
Make 8   *Make 8*

Easy Roofing

The Block Placement Diagram (below), shows two whole house repeats, but only one complete roof. Additional houses are needed to complete the slanting roof sections at the right and left. To streamline the roof assembly, pick 1 roof fabric per house. Cut the roof logs for 4 blocks, and sort into stacks by block. Reassign the 2 stacks for the 2 right-hand blocks to the house on the left.

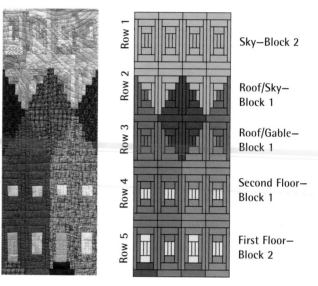

Detail of two houses   *Block Placement Diagram*

Row 1 — Sky—Block 2
Row 2 — Roof/Sky—Block 1
Row 3 — Roof/Gable—Block 1
Row 4 — Second Floor—Block 1
Row 5 — First Floor—Block 2

Note the Log Share between rows 2 and 3; the Roof/Sky blocks in Row 2 are made without a G log at the bottom.

Fabric Key
- muted hues
- grays
- blues
- brights

CAROLINA ROW BLOCK 3 LOG CUTTING GUIDE			
Log	Cut	Width	Length
A	1	2"	2"
B	1	1"	2"
C	1	1"	2½"
D	1	1"	2½"
E	1	1"	3"

Finished Block Size: 2½" x 2½"

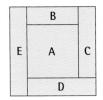
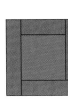

Block 3

*Block 3
Make 46 assorted*

CAROLINA ROW BLOCK 4 LOG CUTTING GUIDE			
Log	Cut	Width	Length
A	1	1½"	1½"
B	1	1"	1½"
C	1	1"	2"
D	1	1"	2"
E	1	1"	2½"
F	1	1"	2½"

Finished Block Size: 2½" x 2½"

Block 4

*Block 4
Make 44 assorted*

ASSEMBLING THE QUILT

For general instructions, see Joining the Blocks (page 41), Making Borders (page 41), and Quilting and Finishing (page 44).

1. Refer to the quilt photograph (page 88) and quilt diagram (page 92). Lay out the blocks in 5 rows of 16 blocks each to make 8 houses total. Double-check the roof alignments and colors. Adjust as needed.

2. Stitch the blocks together in rows. Press. Join the rows. Press.

3. Follow the Border Cutting Guide to cut the inner border strips on the crosswise grain and the outer border strips on the lengthwise grain. Also cut 4 small 1" x 3" filler logs from a roof fabric to be used in the middle borders.

CAROLINA ROW BORDER CUTTING GUIDE				
Border	Fabric	Cut	Width	Length*
inner	yellow	6	1¼"	40"
outer	multicolor	2	2"	44½"
		2	2"	66"

*length is approximate

4. Measure the quilt top to determine the final cut length of the borders. Sew the side inner borders to the quilt top. Press. Sew two strips end to end for both the top and the bottom inner borders. Join the borders to the quilt top. Press.

5. Mix blocks 3 and 4 randomly, not always alternating every other one. Sew the blocks together into 4 strips (the side strips each have 8 of Block 3 and 9 of Block 4; the top and bottom strips each have 15 of Block 3 and 13 of Block 4). Add a filler log to both ends of the side middle border strips. Join the side borders to the quilt. Press. Join the top and bottom middle borders to the quilt, letting the excess extend beyond the quilt at one end. Press. Trim the

overhanging block even with the quilt edge. Add the side outer borders. Press. Add the top and bottom outer borders. Press.

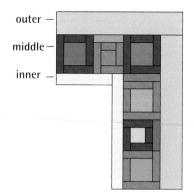

Border Corner Detail

6. Layer and finish the quilt. Use outline quilting to highlight the individual logs in the houses, and diamond grids to depict shingles on the roofs. Quilt gently curved lines meandering through the sky to suggest clouds. Outline-quilt the borders and border blocks near the ditch of the seam. Bind the edges with a 2¼"-wide bias strip cut from a 25" x 25" square of print fabric (see Binding the Quilt, page 45).

Sky quilting detail

Quilt Diagram

Moms and Babes

Moms and Babes, 77½" x 57½", 2002.
Machine-pieced, hand-quilted. Cottons, silk, cotton-polyester blends, cotton brocades, polyester batting.

I enjoy seeing sheep around the world—grazing in front of a castle in Scotland, guided by a shepherd in Spain, resting on a mountainside in Norway. *Moms and Babes* is a wall-sized version of *Morning Graze* (page 6), made to satisfy the many requests I receive for sheep quilt patterns. For inspiration, I once again turned to New Zealand in spring.

This quilt has enough blocks to satisfy anyone desiring "lots of sheep." Don't blame me when you scratch your head trying to figure out the block placement. Even in this scaled-down version, there are more than 300 blocks to keep track of! To ensure that every block found its proper spot, I slipped the quilt diagram into a clear plastic sleeve and wrote individual block numbers on the overlay. I wrote corresponding numbers on removable adhesive labels that I placed on the blocks.

Sizes at a Glance

QUILT: 77½" x 57½"

BLOCK 1: 5" x 2½"

BLOCK 2: 2½" x 2½"

BLOCK 3: 5" x 5"

BLOCK 4: 2½" x 2½"

BLOCK 5: 2½" x 2½"

BLOCK 6: 5" x 10"

BLOCK 7: 5" x 10"

MATERIALS

sky		2 yards total assorted blues
sheep pasture		2 yards total assorted muted greens
sheep		1½ yards total assorted whites
clover field		½ yard total assorted bright greens
tall fescue pasture		½ yard total assorted gray-greens
hillside of Scotch broom		⅜ yard total assorted chartreuse
brown mountain		⅜ yard total assorted browns
purple mountain		⅜ yard total assorted purples
sheep faces		¾ yard total assorted beiges
hoofs, ears, tails		½ yard total assorted blacks
trees		¼ yard total assorted dark greens
inner and outer borders, backing		4⅝ yards purple
middle border		2⅛ yards light print
batting		81" x 61"
bias binding		1 yard

MAKING THE BLOCKS

For general instructions, see Traditional Log Cabin Block (page 22), Offset Center Variation Block (page 24), Cornerstones Log Cabin Block (page 25), Elongated Courthouse Steps (page 27), Small Elongated Courthouse Steps Block (page 28), and Making Blocks (page 38). Follow the log cutting guides and block diagrams to cut and sew the logs. Lay out the logs before you sew them, to ensure the correct orientation. Sort and label the completed blocks. Make 300 blocks total.

MOMS AND BABES BLOCK 1 LOG CUTTING GUIDE

Log	Cut	Width	Length
A	2	1"	1½"
B	2	1"	2½"
C	4	1"	2"
D	2	1"	4½"
E	2	1"	3"

Finished Block Size: 5" x 2½"

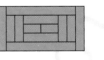

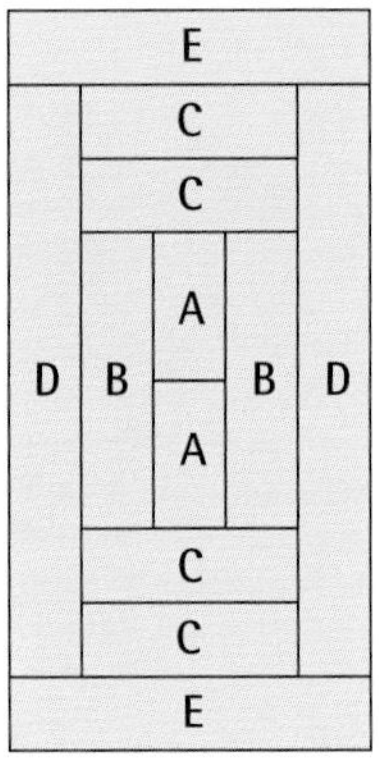

Block 1

Block 1a	*Block 1b*
Make 12	*Make 21*

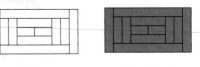

Block 1c	*Block 1d*
Make 15	*Make 11*

Block 1e
Make 2

Block 1f
Make 2

Block 1g
Make 1

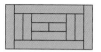

Block 1h
Make 6

Block 1i
Make 3

Block 1j
Make 1

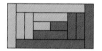

Block 1k
Make 1

Block 1l
Make 1

Block 1m
Make 1

Block 1n
Make 1

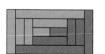

Block 1o
Make 2

Block 1p
Make 1

Block 1q
Make 1

Block 1r
Make 1

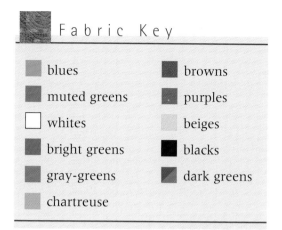

F a b r i c   K e y

- blues
- muted greens
- whites
- bright greens
- gray-greens
- chartreuse
- browns
- purples
- beiges
- blacks
- dark greens

Block 1s
Make 1

Block 1t
Make 1

Block 1u
Make 2

Block 1v
Make 3

Block 1w
Make 3

Precision piecing with two different dark green prints creates the illusion of overlapping pine trees.

Moms and Babes Block 2 Log Cutting Guide

Log	Cut	Width	Length
A	1	1"	1"
B	1	1"	1"
C	1	1"	1½"
D	1	1"	1½"
E	1	1"	2"
F	1	1"	2"
G	1	1"	2½"
H	1	1"	2½"
I	1	1"	3"

Finished Block Size: 2½" x 2½"

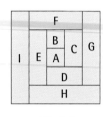

Block 2

Block 2m
Make 3

Block 2n
Make 2

Block 2o
Make 2

Block 2p
Make 2

Block 2q
Make 2

Block 2r
Make 12

Block 2s
Make 1

Block 2t
Make 4

Block 2u
Make 1

Block 2v
Make 2

Block 2w
Make 2

Block 2x
Make 1

Block 2y
Make 1

Block 2z
Make 2

Block 2aa
Make 3
*Trim ½" off Log E and add
a 1" x 1" black cornerstone.*

Block 2bb
Make 1
*Trim ½" off Log G and add
a 1" x 1" black cornerstone.*

Block 2cc
Make 3
*Trim ½" off Log E and add
a 1" x 1" black cornerstone.*

Block 2dd
Make 1
*Trim ½" off Log F and add
a 1" x 1" black cornerstone.*

Block 2ee
Make 2
*Replace Log B with a
1" x 1" black cornerstone.*

Block 2ff
Make 3
*Trim ½" off Log H and add
a 1" x 1" black cornerstone.*

Block 2a
Make 17

Block 2b
Make 23

Block 2c
Make 2

Block 2d
Make 1

Block 2e
Make 18

Block 2f
Make 6

Block 2g
Make 10

Block 2h
Make 13

Block 2i
Make 1

Block 2j
Make 13

Block 2k
Make 3

Block 2l
Make 1

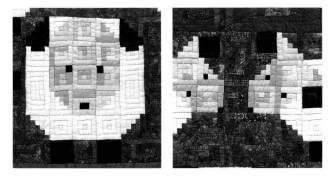

Cornerstones create the faces on Big Mom and her lambs.

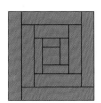

Block 3b
Make 6

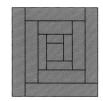

Block 3c
Make 1

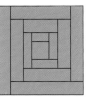

Block 3d
Make 4

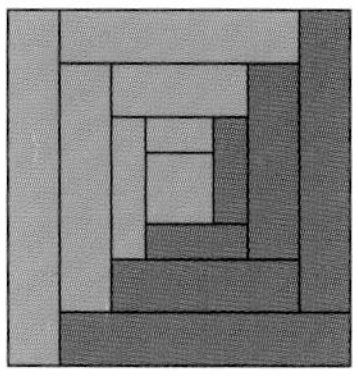

Block 3e
Make 1

MOMS AND BABES BLOCK 3 LOG CUTTING GUIDE

Log	Cut	Width	Length
A	1	1½"	1½"
B	1	1"	1½"
C	1	1"	2"
D	1	1"	2"
E	1	1"	2½"
F	1	1¼"	2½"
G	1	1¼"	3¼"
H	1	1¼"	3¼"
I	1	1¼"	4"
J	1	1¼"	4"
K	1	1¼"	4¾"
L	1	1¼"	4 ¾"
M	1	1¼"	5½"

Finished Block Size: 5" x 5"

MOMS AND BABES BLOCK 4 LOG CUTTING GUIDE

Log	Cut	Width	Length
A	1	1¼"	1¼"
B	1	1"	1¼"
C	1	1"	1¾"
D	1	1¼"	1¾"
E	1	1¼"	1¼"
F	1	1¼"	1¾"
G	1	1"	2½"
H	1	1"	3"

Finished Block Size: 2½" x 2½"

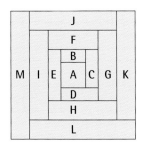

Block 3

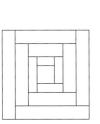

Block 3a
Make 11

Block 4

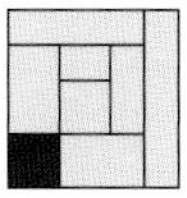

Block 4
Make 8

MOMS AND BABES BLOCK 5 LOG CUTTING GUIDE

Log	Cut	Width	Length
A	1	1¼"	1½"
B	1	1"	1½"
C	2	1¼"	1¾"
D	1	1"	3"
E	1	1¼"	3"

Finished Block Size: 2½" x 2½"

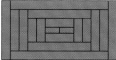

Block 6a
Make 8

Block 6b
Make 1

Block 6c
Make 2

Block 6d
Make 1

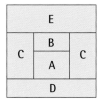

Block 5

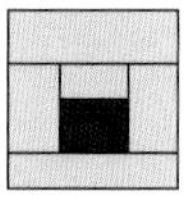

Block 5
Make 4

MOMS AND BABES BLOCK 7 LOG CUTTING GUIDE

Log	Cut	Width	Length
A	2	1½"	1½"
B	2	1"	2½"
C	2	1½"	2½"
D	2	1"	4½"
E	2	1½"	3½"
F	2	1"	6½"
G	2	1½"	4½"
H	2	1"	8 ½"
I	2	1½"	5½"

Finished Block Size: 5" x 10"

MOMS AND BABES BLOCK 6 LOG CUTTING GUIDE

Log	Cut	Width	Length
A	2	1"	1¾"
B	2	1¼"	3"
C	4	1¼"	2½"
D	2	1¼"	6"
E	4	1¼"	4"
F	2	1¼"	9"
G	2	1¼"	5½"

Finished Block Size: 5" x 10"

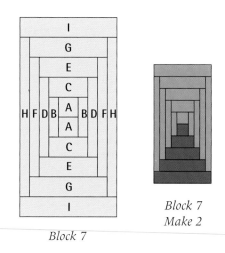

Block 7

Block 7
Make 2

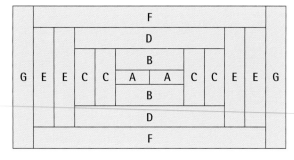

Block 6

ASSEMBLING THE QUILT

For general instructions, see Joining the Blocks (page 41), Making Borders (page 41), and Quilting and Finishing (page 44).

1. Lay out 300 blocks to create the sheep pasture scene, as shown in the quilt photograph (page 93) and quilt diagram (page 100). Carefully match the orientation—many blocks are rotated left, right, or upside down. View your layout through a reducing glass to locate any blocks that are upside-down, out of place, or incorrectly pieced. Make corrections as needed.

2. Follow the assembly diagram to sew the blocks together in sections. Start with the smallest blocks in each section, pressing as you go. Continue adding on and/or joining smaller units together until the section is complete. If possible, plan the pressing sequence so that the seams will butt when several units or sections are joined. Make 7 sections for Row 1, 12 sections for Row 2, and 9 sections for Row 3. Follow the numbers to join the sections into rows. Press. Join the rows together. Press.

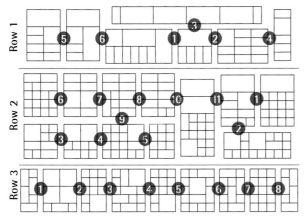

Assembly Diagram

3. Follow the Border Cutting Guide to cut the border fabrics into lengthwise strips. Measure the quilt top to determine the final cut length of the borders.

MOMS AND BABES BORDER CUTTING GUIDE				
Border	Fabric	Cut	Width	Length*
inner	purple	2	1½"	70½"
		2	1½"	52½"
middle	light print	2	1½"	72½"
		2	1½"	54½"
outer	purple	2	2"	74½"
		2	2"	57½"

*length is approximate

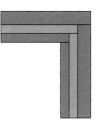

Border Corner Detail

4. Join the top and bottom inner border strips to the quilt top. Press. Join the side inner border strips to the quilt top. Press. Join the middle and outer border strips in the same sequence, pressing after each addition.

5. Layer and finish the quilt. To depict woolly sheep coats, quilt the sheep blocks near the ditch of the seam, starting at the outside and spiraling in toward the center. Quilt contour lines on the mountains and diagonal lines on the trees. Quilt the sky in free-flowing lines. Quilt blades of grass in the pastures and fields. Bind the edges with a 2¼"-wide bias strip cut from a 27" x 27" square of the fabric of your choice (see Binding the Quilt, page 45).

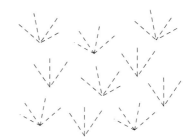

Grass Quilting Design

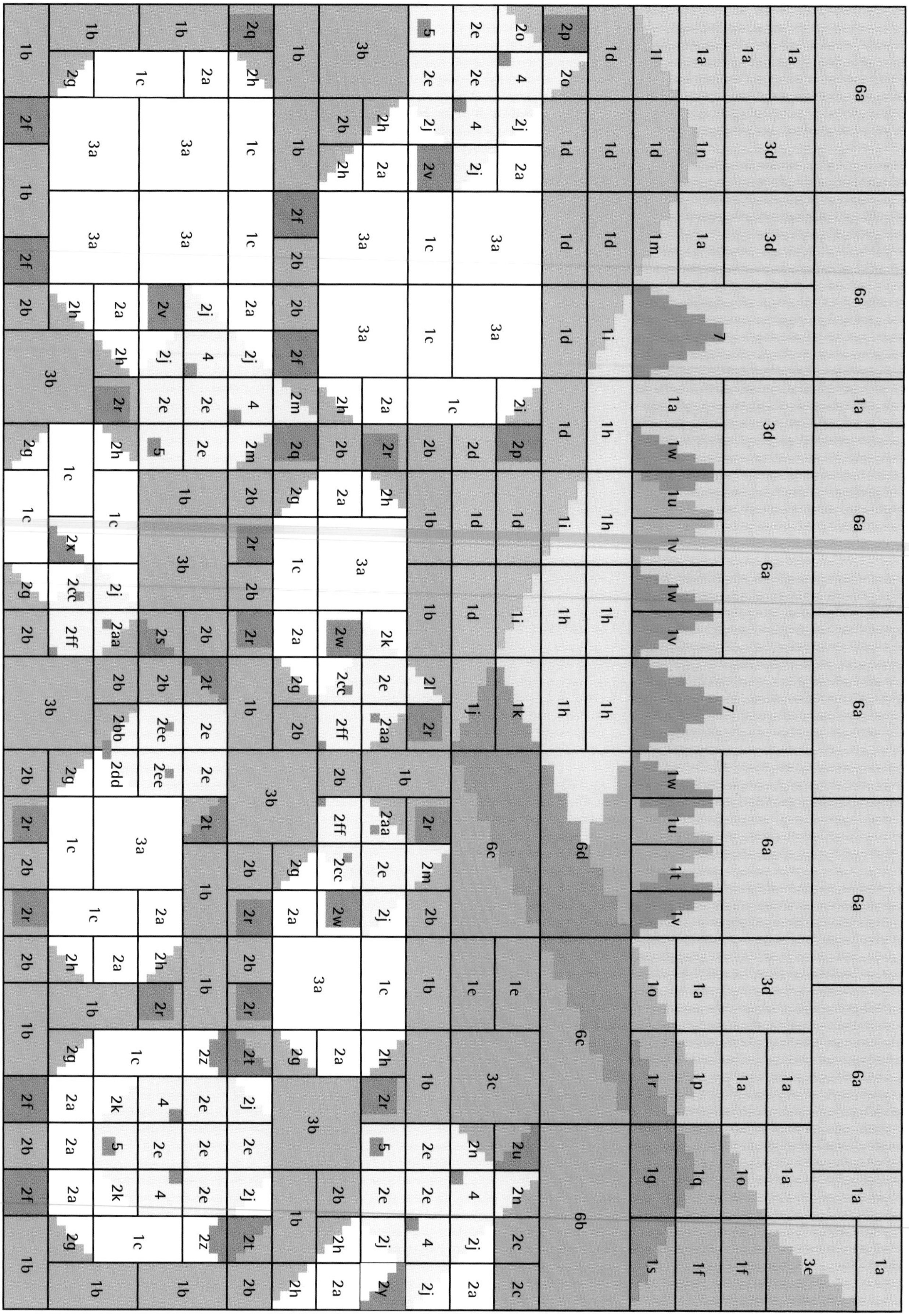

Quilt Diagram

Canterbury Fields

Canterbury Fields, 78½" x 68½", 1998.
Machine-pieced, hand-quilted. Cottons, polyester batting.

Our three trips to New Zealand have generated hundreds of colorful slides. Dozens of New Zealand's awesome natural sights routinely vie for my attention and selection as a design source. A postcard view of the Canterbury Plains won this time around. This exciting aerial view simultaneously posed a challenge and a solution. Since the fields already looked like Crazy-Patch piecing, why not make them that way? The finished quilt uses two different patchwork techniques: Log Cabin blocks for the mountains and sky, and Crazy-Patch for the fields.

Sizes
at a Glance

QUILT: 78½" x 68½"
BLOCK 1: 10" x 5"
BLOCK 2: 5" x 5"
BLOCK 3: 10" x 5"

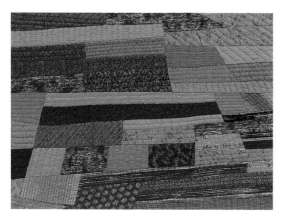

Detail of fields. To make the Crazy-Patch pattern, the line drawing was enlarged using an overhead projector.

MATERIALS

sky ▦ 1½ yards total assorted blue prints and solids

clouds, snowcaps ☐ ½ yard total assorted whites

mountains, riverbank ◪◪▦ 2 yards total assorted grays, gray-browns, dark browns

riverbed ½ yard mottled rust/gray/brown print

fields 3 yards total assorted greens, golds, tans, browns

border strips ⅔ yard green

2⅛ yards gold decorative print

½ yard brown

backing 5 yards

batting 82" x 72"

bias binding 1 yard

You'll also need:
 an overhead projector
 (or visit a drafting or copy center)
 large wall space
 2 yards muslin or white fabric
 chart paper or freezer paper
 transparency film

Fabric notes: The mountain fabrics in *Canterbury Fields* are close in value and print scale to imply distance and similarity. If you want more distinctive mountain peaks and valleys, use solids or extend the value scales in the palette. Subtle stripes and small linear prints make excellent field rows and furrows. These fabrics can be cut lengthwise, crosswise, and on the diagonal for variety.

Detail of mountains and sky

MAKING THE BLOCKS

For general instructions, see Traditional Log Cabin Block (page 22), Elongated Courthouse Steps Block (page 27), and Making Blocks (page 38). Each block in this design can be divided diagonally into four V-shaped quadrants. All of the logs in a quadrant are cut from the same fabric to create a distinct color fill in that area. Center logs can belong to any quadrant. The scene takes shape when the finished blocks are joined together. To begin, select one fabric for each mountain, referring to the quilt diagram (page 107). The sky and cloud fabrics vary within each block. Follow the log cutting guides and block diagrams to make 44 blocks total. To keep track of your progress, lay a sheet of clear plastic on the grid and number the blocks 1–44 with a permanent marker. Check off the blocks on the overlay as you complete them.

CANTERBURY FIELDS BLOCK 1 LOG CUTTING GUIDE			
Log	Cut	Width	Length
A	2	1½"	1½"
B	2	1"	2½"
C	2	1½"	2½"
D	2	1"	4½"
E	2	1½"	3½"
F	2	1"	6½"
G	2	1½"	4½"
H	2	1"	8½"
I	2	1½"	5½"

Finished Block Size: 10" x 5"

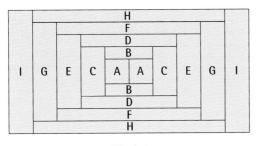

Block 1

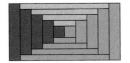

Quadrants

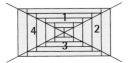

Block 1a
Make 8 sky blocks
and 2 assorted mountains

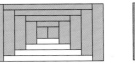

Block 1b
Make 5

Block 1c
Make 3
assorted mountains

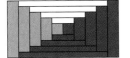

Block 1d
Make 1

Block 1e
Make 1

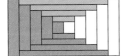

Block 1f
Make 1

Block 1g
Make 1

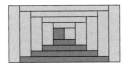

Block 1h
Make 1

Block 1i
Make 1

Block 1j
Make 1

Block 1k
Make 1

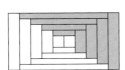

Block 1l
Make 1

CANTERBURY FIELDS BLOCK 2 LOG CUTTING GUIDE

Log	Cut	Width	Length
A	1	1½"	1½"
B	1	1"	1½"
C	1	1½"	2"
D	1	1½"	2½"
E	1	1"	3"
F	1	1½"	3"
G	1	1"	4"
H	1	1"	3½"
I	1	1½"	4½"
J	1	1"	4½"
K	1	1"	5"
L	1	1"	5"
M	1	1"	5½"

Finished Block Size: 5" x 5"

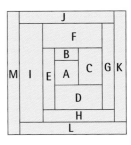

Block 2

Quadrants

Block 2a
Make 2 assorted
mountains

Block 2b
Make 1

Block 2c
Make 1

CANTERBURY FIELDS BLOCK 3 LOG CUTTING GUIDE

Log	Cut	Width	Length
A	2	1"	1¾"
B	1	1¼"	3"
C	2	1¼"	1¾"
D	1	1¼"	4½"
E	4	1¼"	2½"
F	2	1¼"	7½"
G	3	1¼"	4"
H	1	1¼"	9¾"
I	1	1¼"	4¾"
J	1	1¼"	10½"

Finished Block Size: 10" x 5"

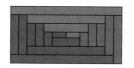

Block 3c
Make 1

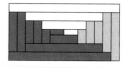

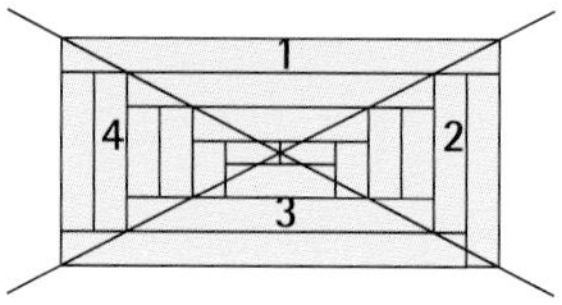

Block 3d
Make 1

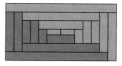

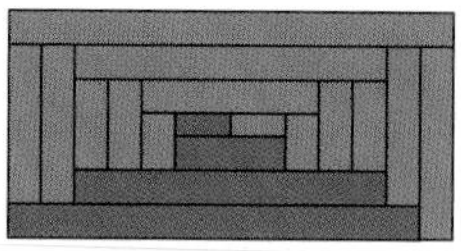

Block 3e
Make 1

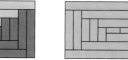

Block 3f
Make 1

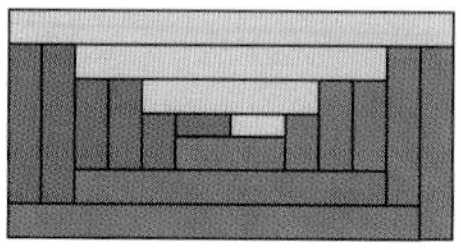

Block 3g
Make 1

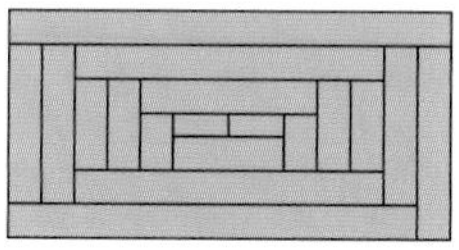

Block 3h
Make 1

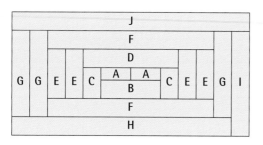

Block 3

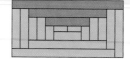

Block 3i
Make 1

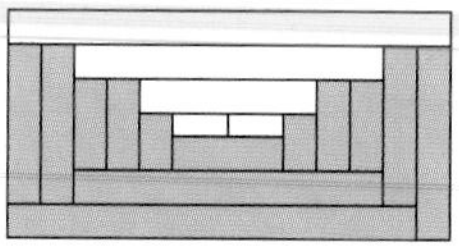

Block 3j
Make 1

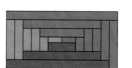

Quadrants

Block 3k
Make 1

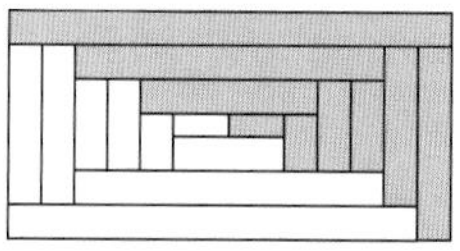

Block 3l
Make 1

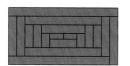

Block 3a
Make 2
assorted mountains

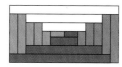

Block 3b
Make 1

Fabric Key

- blues
- whites
- grays
- gray/browns
- dark brown

MAKING THE PATCHWORK FIELDS

1. Tape or tack the muslin or white fabric to a wall. Trace the field diagram/pattern (page 107) on the transparency film. Use an overhead projector to project the transparency drawing onto the fabric, adjusting so that the fields measure 72" across. Mark the field, river, and riverbank outlines on the fabric. This enlarged drawing is your master pattern. (Alternatively, enlarge the pattern to 72" wide on a wide-format photocopier at a drafting or photocopy shop.)

2. To make individual templates, unroll chart paper or freezer paper, shiny side up, over the master pattern, and tape, tack, or pin in place. Trace the field, river, and riverbank outlines with a permanent marker. Number each piece on the template drawing. Turn the template drawing over. Transfer the numbers to the back, mark a north (top) arrow on each field, and mark indicator ticks across adjacent fields, to aid the alignment during piecing. Cut the templates apart on the marked lines. Reattach the templates to the master pattern, and number the master to correspond.

Mark the field number, a north (top) arrow, and tick marks on the reverse side of every field template.

3. Select a fabric for each field, auditioning for color and value contrast. Turn the fabric right side down. Place the field template shiny side down on top, orienting it along the lengthwise grain, unless the fabric stripe or print suggests a different placement. Press the freezer paper template lightly with a warm iron until the shiny side adheres to the fabric. If using chart paper, pin the paper template to the fabric. Mark a sewing line on the fabric by tracing around the template with a contrasting colored pencil. Cut ¼" beyond the template edge to create a seam allowance. Label the right side of the fabric piece (using a self-adhesive removable label) to make tracking and positioning easier. Reattach the piece to the master pattern. Continue until all the field pieces are cut.

4. Place two adjacent fields right sides together, aligning the tick marks. Don't remove the templates unless they are in the way. Stitch on the marked line, using a ¼" seam. Press. Continue stitching the various fields together, section by section. The pattern contains numerous straight seams that are easy to sew. When pivots are necessary, leave ¼" unsewn at the ends of seams. Save very long, straight seams for joining large sections when you assemble the quilt. Periodically position the pieced field sections on the master pattern to check their layout, orientation, and accuracy. Keep the templates attached to the outer edges of the pieced panel for stability.

5. Select fabrics for the riverbed and riverbank. Repeat the Step 3 technique to mark and cut these large pieces for each template. Repeat the Step 4 technique to align and sew the riverbed and riverbank pieces to each other. Piece the upper edge of the bank to the upper fields. Piece the lower edge of the river to the fields on both sides of the sharp curve. Press seams toward the river. Turn under the curve and appliqué by hand.

6. Realign the completed patchwork on the master pattern. Pin in place. Turn the work over. Make a straight cut along the top edge. Trim the remaining edges so that the patchwork panel measures 70½" x 30½".

ASSEMBLING THE QUILT

For general instructions, see Joining the Blocks (page 41), Making Borders (page 41), and Quilting and Finishing (page 44).

1. Lay out the blocks in 6 rows to create the sky and mountains landscape, as shown in the quilt photograph (page 101) and quilt block diagram (page 107). Note that rows 1–5 have 7 blocks each but that Row 6 has 9 blocks.

2. Stitch the blocks together in rows. Press. Join the rows. Press.

3. Stitch the top of the patchwork fields to the base of the Log Cabin panel. Press.

4. Follow the Border Cutting Guide to cut the border fabrics into strips. Cut the green strips crosswise and sew them end to end in pairs; repeat with the brown strips. Cut the gold strips lengthwise. Measure the quilt top to determine the final cut length of the borders.

CANTERBURY FIELDS BORDER CUTTING GUIDE				
Border	Fabric	Cut	Width	Length*
inner, outer accent	green	16	1¼"	40"
decorative	gold	2	2"	72"
		2	2"	65"
outer	brown	8	1½"	40"

*length is approximate

5. Sew the top and bottom inner accent borders to the quilt. Press. Sew the side inner accent borders to the quilt. Press. Add the decorative borders, outer accent borders, and outer borders in the same way, pressing after each addition.

Border Corner Diagram

6. Layer and finish the quilt. Refer to the Canterbury Fields Quilting Sample for quilting ideas for the sky, mountains, and fields. The snow-peaked mountains include snowflake designs. The quilting design motif on the dry riverbed fabric depicts large stones. Outline-quilt near the ditch in the border strips. Quilt the repetitive decorative motif in the gold border. The pattern isn't dense, so shadow-quilt this same motif in the border's open areas. Bind the edges with a 2¼"-wide bias strip cut from a 27" x 27" square of the fabric of your choice (see Binding the Quilt, page 45).

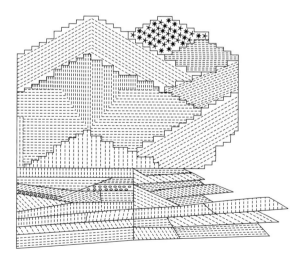

Canterbury Fields Quilting Sample

1b	1a	1b	1a	1a	1b	1a
1a	1a	1a	1b	3h*	1a	1b
1e	1h	1l	3i*	3j*	1k	3l*
1c	3d	3b	1i	1f	3f	1j
3a	1a	1d	3g	3k*	1g	3e
1c	3c	2a / 2c	1a	1c	3a	2b / 2a

*rotate block 180°

Quilt Blocks Diagram

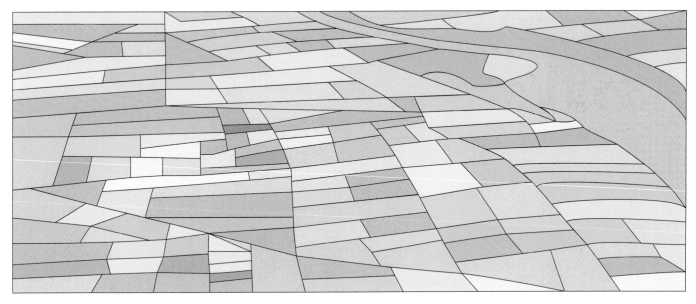

Field Diagram/Pattern

Looking Back:
A Retrospective of Forerunner Quilts

This retrospective gallery spans a quarter century of my work. Each quilt depicts an image, shape, or scene. I've turned many of my trial-and-error design experiments into learning and teaching tools for my classes. Students are amused to see the limited palette of cotton fabrics we had available in 1979, when I created *Mountains and Meadows*. From that standpoint, 1970s-era quilts are fast becoming archival. When a design inspiration didn't lend itself exclusively to Log Cabin piecing, I allowed myself the liberty of branching out into other areas. I also included quilts that use simple, repeated patchwork blocks to create a design grid.

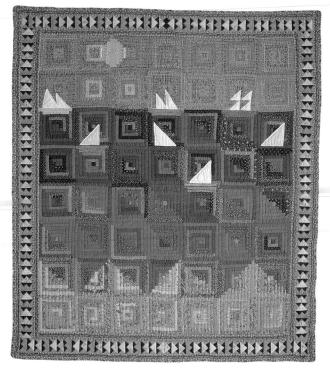

Seascape, 72" x 78", 1979.
Traditional Log Cabin blocks with Flying Geese border. Machine-pieced, hand-quilted. Cottons and cotton-polyester blends, polyester batting. Original design sketch by Glenn Glover.

BELOW: Sailboat on Puget Sound, Washington, with Mt. Rainier barely visible in background.

Mt. Bachelor in central Oregon with a grassy meadow in the foreground.

Mountains and Meadows, 78" x 62", 1979.
Traditional and Offset Center Log Cabin blocks. Machine-pieced, hand-quilted. Cottons and cotton-polyester blends, polyester batting. Original design sketch by Glenn Glover.

Turning the blocks on point intensifies the setting sun.

Red sky at night, sailors' delight.

A Christmas tree farm in brilliant white snow inspired a quilt of stylized trees.

Sailors' Delight, 66" x 66", 1984.
Rail Fence blocks with sailboat border. Machine-pieced, hand-quilted. Cottons and cotton-polyester blends, polyester batting.

Rainbow Connection, 64" x 64", 1980.
Traditional Log Cabin blocks. Machine-pieced, hand-quilted. Cottons and cotton-polyester blends, polyester batting. The colorful rainbow extends into border crossbars, inspiring the quilt's name. Puffy white clouds are randomly placed.

White Christmas, 52" x 50", 1990.
Triangular Log Cabin blocks. Machine-pieced, hand-quilted.
Cottons, polyester batting.
Inset: White beads and clear rosettes resemble miniature white lights.

Fourth Forest:
A Story Quilt

In the late nineteenth and early twentieth centuries, lumber companies practiced a "cut out and get out" philosophy, moving from New England to the Lake States to the South, as they depleted the standing timber supply. But before they could "get out" of the South, the forest regrew on its own! Many companies stayed to harvest the second-growth timber.

Scientific forest management in the late 1940s and early 1950s led to a third harvest in the 1970s and 1980s. With sound management and protection from wildfires, the South's "fourth forest" began to thrive and mature. Today, in some places, even a "fifth forest" is being managed. All southern states have more acres of forestland than fifty years ago. The quilt, *Fourth Forest*, acknowledges the success of modern sustainable forest-management practices.

Quilted leaves (back view).

Fall's Glow, 76" x 62", 1986.
Kaleidoscope blocks. Machine-pieced, hand-quilted. Cottons and cotton-polyester blends, polyester batting. Colorful mix of hardwoods and pines in autumn fill a kaleidoscope patchwork grid.

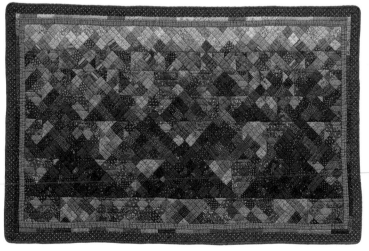

Fourth Forest, 57" x 36", 1986.
One-Patch and Half-Square triangles. Machine-pieced, hand-quilted. Cottons and cotton-polyester blends, polyester batting. Images higher in the horizontal plane appear more distant. Repetition and color play also advance the depth. Trees become progressively smaller as they fade into the horizon.

Hemlocks, 52" x 60", 1985.
Rail Fence blocks. Machine-pieced, hand-quilted. Cottons and cotton-polyester blends, polyester batting. A Rail Fence grid was used to design stylized trees randomly scattered on a light background.

FOR FURTHER READING

Barnes, Christine. Color: *The Quilters Guide.* Bothell, WA: That Patchwork Place, Inc., 1997.

Colvin, Joan. *Quilts From Nature.* Bothell, WA: That Patchwork Place, Inc., 1993.

Hall, Jane, and Dixie Haywood. *Firm Foundations.* Paducah, KY: American Quilter's Society, 1996.

Hall, Jane, and Dixie Haywood. *Hall and Haywood's Foundation Quilts: Building on the Past.* Paducah, KY: American Quilter's Society, 2000.

Martin, Judy. *Judy Martin's Ultimate Rotary Cutting Reference.* Grinnell, IA: Crosley-Griffith Corp., 1997.

McClun, Diana, and Laura Nownes. *Quilts, Quilts, and More Quilts!* Lafayette, CA: C&T Publishing, 1993.

McDowell, Ruth B. *Piecing: Expanding the Basics.* Lafayette, CA: C&T Publishing, 1998.

Quilter's Newsletter Magazine, Quiltmaker Magazine, and C&T Publishing. *All About Quilting from A to Z.* Lafayette, CA: C&T Publishing, 2002.

INDEX

Boldface page references indicate quilt photographs.

ABOUT THE AUTHOR

Flavin Glover grew up in Cullman County, Alabama, falling asleep each night under the string patchwork quilts made by her mom, Nonnie Williams. Nonnie eventually taught Flavin the essentials of scrap quilting, but only when Flavin demonstrated her interest was genuine. After graduating from college in the mid-1970s, Flavin undertook quilting with two goals in mind. One was to learn patchwork techniques and include them in the arts and crafts therapy classes she taught. Another was to use up the fabric scraps she had accumulated while a student majoring in Clothing, Textiles and Related Arts at Auburn University.

Flavin's interests include gardening and creative cooking. Flavin is a two-time Pillsbury Bake Off winner, and her cooking played a role in her becoming a nationally recognized quilt artist and teacher. While Flavin was in Miami for the 1980 Bake Off, coordinators of the Tropical Florida Quilt Conference asked her to return later that year to teach. Since then, Flavin has given presentations and taught workshops throughout the country.

Flavin's originally designed quilts of geometric patchwork and everchanging Log Cabin blocks are filled with numerous fabrics in vibrant colors. Her patchwork quilts and wearable fashions have been published and exhibited extensively since 1979.

Flavin, her husband, Glenn, and their three cats, Patch, Oreo, and Gracie, live in the college town of Auburn, Alabama. Glenn is a professor in the School of Forestry and Wildlife Sciences at Auburn University. The couple's mutual hobbies include traveling, photography, and cross-country skiing. Together they have participated in volunteer construction teams in Central and South America, often in remote villages.

Flavin has met one of her two self-imposed goals—that of learning how to quilt. She hasn't done as well at using up her scraps. Comparing the amount of fabric she owns to her projected life expectancy, it's not looking good. But one goal out of two isn't bad!

For more information on other C&T books, write or call for a free catalog:

C&T Publishing, Inc.
P.O. Box 1456
Lafayette, CA 94549
(800) 284-1114
Email: ctinfo@ctpub.com
Website: www.ctpub.com

Note: Fabrics used in the quilts shown may not be currently available since fabric manufacturers keep most fabrics in print for only a short time.

For quilting supplies:

Cotton Patch Mail Order
3405 Hall Lane, Dept.CTB
Lafayette, CA 94549
(800) 835-4418
(925) 283-7883
Email:quiltusa@yahoo.com
Website: www.quiltusa.com